Ellen's Story

Thank you for helping
those who so badly
need it,

Hugs Ellen Szita

Ellen Szita

Order this book online at www.trafford.com/07-0533
or email orders@trafford.com

Most Trafford titles are also available at major online book retailers.

Note for Librarians: A cataloguing record for this book is available from Library
and Archives Canada at www.collectionscanada.ca/amicus/index-e.html

Printed in Victoria, BC, Canada.

ISBN: 978-1-4251-2129-7

*We at Trafford believe that it is the responsibility of us all, as both individuals
and corporations, to make choices that are environmentally and socially sound.
You, in turn, are supporting this responsible conduct each time you purchase a
Trafford book, or make use of our publishing services. To find out how you are
helping, please visit www.trafford.com/responsiblepublishing.html*

*Our mission is to efficiently provide the world's finest, most comprehensive
book publishing service, enabling every author to experience success.
To find out how to publish your book, your way, and have it available
worldwide, visit us online at www.trafford.com/10510*

 www.trafford.com

North America & international
toll-free: 1 888 232 4444 (USA & Canada)
phone: 250 383 6864 ♦ fax: 250 383 6804 ♦ email: info@trafford.com

The United Kingdom & Europe
phone: +44 (0)1865 722 113 ♦ local rate: 0845 230 9601
facsimile: +44 (0)1865 722 868 ♦ email: info.uk@trafford.com

10 9 8 7 6 5 4 3 2

Contents

<u>Acknowledgement</u>

I would like to acknowledge;

Joan Van Dyke for the editing of this book

-

The READ Society for their undying devotion and patience in giving me the foundation to a new way of life.

-

Melanie Austin my teacher, friend and mentor

-

Andreas my son-in-law who spent many hours helping me, get this book on the road.

Chris Hinz, my photographer and make up artist.

And to,

My four children,
Kim, Anthony, Robert, Carolann
& my son-in-law Jason

And

My five Grandchildren,
Jenna, Shantelle, Jordon, Anthony and Sheena,

Who, without their undying love and support, this book could not have been possible?

To all of you I say thank you for making my dream come true.

Dedication

I dedicate this story to,

My Mother and Father

My brother Billy

My niece Heidi and her
Four children

And Kelly.

God Says Set Them Free

The winds have blown you faraway
but the love in your voices are here to stay.

I hear you speak when the wind comes calling.
I hear you through the winter leaf's falling.

I see you in the glistening sun, your mast upon the
sea.
I miss you all so very much but God says, to set
you free.

Ellen Szita

PREFACE

"Ellen's Story" is a testament of my persistent struggle for literacy, the crippling defeat I suffered in my adult life due to this problem, and the ultimate steps I needed to take toward triumph.

My story begins in England as World War II breaks out. As a victim of the times and of a society unaware of learning disabilities, I fell further and further behind in a system focused on only achievers. At the age of 18, contemplating a dim future as an ill-educated factory worker and bearing thoughts of suicide, I immigrated to Canada. But dreams of a new life of marriage, children and friendships never came to be; struggles with learning disabilities sabotaged every hope. My marriage failed, I sunk into a deep depression, and I tried to raise four children on welfare. Eventually, after intensive therapy, I was diagnosed with dyslexia and only grade 7 reading skills. Through the incredible support from the Victoria READ Society, a special school in B.C., I came to believe I could learn, and learn I did.

However, my triumphs came with more pain. Literacy problems had devastated my life and my relationships, and I felt an incredible fear knowing the lives I'd hurt. But then I learned I was far from alone; there were millions in Canada that were feeling the same shame and hopelessness that I was.

What was the true number of people – particularly children – suffering as a result of this issue?

Expressing these concerns and trying to stop this devastating cycle became my passion. I joined civic, provincial and even federal literacy movements. I began speaking at schools, universities, local organizations, prisons and conferences. I published poetry and short stories and wrote articles for newspapers and magazines. I gave workshops for teachers, social workers, doctors, administrators, and government officials, and I lobbied for literacy on Parliament Hill.

"A Day in the Life of a Year," Peter Gzowski's article about my literacy problems and the devastation it caused me, was published in Canadian Living Magazine in 1991 and drew attention to the issue. The following year the award-winning Robert Duncan's documentary "Ellen's Story" was released to international acclaim. This very public exposure forced me to relive my painful childhood at school. But parts were missing because I had not healed enough to tell the whole story at that time. Since then I have found the courage to tell all in my book.

The terrible effects of literacy and numerous problems on human health, wealth and happiness are unseen. The victims face lifelong shame, guilt and failure. I hope my story will open eyes to the real destruction of this hidden epidemic and give courage to those willing to come forward and attend classes. But more importantly, since less than 5% of adults with learning difficulties seek help, I hope my story will give courage and hope to others.

Low literacy is a growing concern in industrialized countries as the demand of the work force and global economy changes. Organizations, agencies and individuals at all levels have begun to seek solutions. I hope that my book will add an important and often unheard voice to the discussions and for the many voices of Adult Learners in communities around the world who live in silent darkness.

CHAPTER 1

Daisies Beside The Train Tracks

I remember clearly the day we arrived at our new home; it was shortly after the Second World War, August 8, 1948, my sister Sylvia's birthday. She was seven, a year younger than me. My parents moved from downtown Brighton into the country. However, we would still be living in Brighton, Sussex. It was strange having my father home. He had been in the navy most of his life but when the war ended he left.

The new house was beautiful, with a garden both back and front. Once inside the house, I ran to the top of stairs and peered out the window that faced the front of the house. I was in awe at being in the country. There were cows in the field directly across from us, and at the bottom of the road was a tunnel. As I watched a train pass over the top the noise from the steam engine, the blowing of the whistle and the puffs of smoke made my skin tingle. For a while, I watched the movers bringing in the furniture. Then I heard my sister Sylvia calling, "Ellen, let's go into the fields."

Big beautiful daisies that came up to our knees bloomed all along the embankment of the train tracks. They were the largest I'd ever seen, and the fields below were full of buttercups and clovers and various other wild flowers. The smell was wonderful, quite different from the ocean air we were used to. Sylvia and I sat making daisy chains. Laughing, she put one on her head. Her hair was a lighter brown than mine. I always thought of her as a porcelain doll, her face pale and shiny. We spent many happy days in these fields, and on occasion, as the train went by, the fireman would blow his whistle and wave. It made me feel special.

My sister Ann was the oldest, then came Billy, who was two years older than me. I was eight at the time. Sylvia was next then Bobby, who was five, and

Joan, three. We all had straight dark hair and dark eyes, except Bobby, who was a complete contrast to the rest of us. He had very curly blonde hair with striking blue eyes and a freckled face.

Billy, Sylvia, Bobby and I often went into the woods and climbed my favorite tree. This tree stood out from all the others because it was dead. But its huge trunk and big branches seemed to invite me. Over the next few years, I climbed to the top many times, giving myself a feeling of accomplishment, something I rarely felt. One day Billy took out his penknife and carved a heart into the tree with an arrow through it, putting our initials inside.

Grandma, my mother's mum, came to live with us at Ashurst Road, shortly after we had moved into our new home. At first I was thrilled because I'd missed her. My fondest memory of her was when we'd be on our way to school. She'd be waiting at the end of Kingswood Flats, which is where we lived during the war, to give us sweets, 'boo boos' as she called them. She'd tell us not to let mother know because it meant Grandma used all her sugar rations on us. But the sad truth was Granny was very sick with cancer. I hadn't been sure my mother loved anyone except my sister Ann, but I was wrong. She loved her mother deeply and nursed her lovingly until she went into the hospital. Grandma died shortly afterwards. She was only sixty-three. Mother stopped singing after Granny died. I missed hearing her lovely voice. Perhaps that's when I first noticed things were not good at home. Mum said Dad missed the navy and had a very difficult time adjusting to all of us children. There were six of us under the age of ten. He would get angry with us for every little thing. If one item on the mantelpiece was moved just the slightest bit to one side, he'd notice. We had to keep our shoes clean at all times and in a neat row. Anyone who forgot would be pulled out of bed no matter what the hour was. Ann used to say it was because he had to be very tidy aboard ship, so we had to be the same. If we forgot to wash our hands before meals, we'd get our face slapped. And those who didn't finish everything on their plate upset Dad the most. He would be furious if we left any doors open in the winter, especially the one to the front room. That was the only room where Mum kept a fire going. The rest of the house was left freezing. I suffered with cramps at the back of my legs. But Sylvia suffered even more with chilblains on her toes. They would be red and swollen and it wasn't unusual to see her limping in the winter.

We did hear stories of how Dad suffered as a child and during the war. We would hear Mum talking to his shipmates that came to visit, and they talked of a time when Dad was on a Russian convoy. It was in the middle of winter, and they were engaged in battle. His hands kept sticking to the gun - even with his gloves on, and he had icicles on his beard and eyebrows. As for his childhood, I knew he starved many times. He was the oldest of five, and he was born out of wedlock. His mother did eventually marry but not Dad's father. She married a widower with two children. He was a chronic alcoholic and very abusive both physically and sexually. Father, being the oldest, felt responsible for feeding his siblings. So, late at night, he would go through the wealthy neighborhoods and look for food in the garbage cans. Fridges were unheard of in homes at that time, and that meant the wealthy threw out the leftovers at the end of the day. He'd go hunting for wood because they couldn't afford to put coal on the fire. Of what I heard about my dad and his suffering, I could write book. He talked very little even when he was angry; it was his face that told you to run for cover. If I know anything at all about my dad it was that he loved the navy and hated leaving it. I think the discipline he received in the navy he actually loved. I heard Mum say once that it put his life in order. I didn't really understand that.

Dad started working in a factory. Mum took charge of the money and spent hours trying to figure it out. I watched her struggle with math as I did. She worried sick about money and kept every penny in her handbag. And even if she went to the lavatory, she would take her purse with her. Much like Dad, Mum had starved as a child too. That must have been a great worry for Mother having to feed all of us. Dad kept a lock on the pantry stopping us from snacking between meals.

Over the next couple of years, I watched Dad progressively get angrier. He took to keeping a cane on the ledge above the living room door. Mum used his bad temper as a weapon to make us behave.

Billy, my brother, had dark, thick hair, full lips and Dad's strong nose. I always looked up to Billy and never understood why Dad treated him as he did. Billy couldn't do anything right, according to Dad. From what I saw, Billy suffered the most from Dad's temper. On one occasion, father was so furious with Billy, he threw the vacuum cleaner at him. Billy was about eleven at the time. Aunt Rose was living with us when this incident took place. She ran to protect Billy from the vacuum, and it hit her instead, breaking her arm. Another time Billy went into Dad's shed and took two treacle tins that Dad was saving. Someone at school had shown Billy how to make a telephone by putting string through the bottom of the tins. I was never sure how it worked, but Billy was fascinated by the idea and had to try it. He was always trying to make things and generally successful at what ever he attempted. This particular night Dad went to the shed, and even though there were lots of tins, he noticed that two were missing. My father went up the stairs to Billy's bedroom where he was playing with Bobby and the tins. My father grabbed the two tins and bent them on Billy's head. I could hear my little brother Bobby screaming. I stood at the bottom of the stairs frozen. At that moment, Aunt Rose who lived with us came home from work. On hearing the screaming, she ran up the stairs. She started yelling at my father, "Are you insane? Look what you have done to your own son." Still standing at the bottom of the stairs looking up at the landing, I saw my Aunty appear with Billy holding his head with one hand while wrap- ping her other arm around his shoulder. I couldn't see Billy's face for the blood. Aunt Rose took him to the hospital. The rest of the evening Father remained silent and dismayed as I was over Billy, I felt an inexplicable compassion for my dad when he went quiet. I felt he was riddled with guilt, and remorse; even worse, that he didn't know why he reacted that way. But I think his heartbreak was, not knowing how to stop. Sometimes I'd see a certain look on Dad's face, as though he were in a fog desperately trying to find a clearing.

Whenever I was sad, I'd take off over the fields or go through to the woods to the other side where there was a pond with frogs, big beautiful blue dragonflies and other strange water creatures, all new to me.

Ann was attending a high school close to where we lived; she was so lucky. It was a new school, and it had a gym with showers. Ann loved school, but then she was in a B-class throughout her entire schooling. I liked the thought that she was clever because it gave me some pride, even if it was for Ann. Anyway, I loved her very much. When she took care of us, which she did a lot, she always made the day so exiting. Either we went to the beach or on a picnic or sometimes we would sneak into the community swimming pool so we wouldn't have to pay.

Sylvia and I hated our school. St. Joseph's was in desperate need of repair. One day in Sylvia's class, part of the ceiling fell down. No one was hurt, but it terrified Sylvia; they let Sylvia stay with me for the rest of the day because it was the only way she would stop crying. Each day the canteen food arrived in big silver containers, and it tasted rotten, as though it had been in those containers forever. Sylvia was always being scolded by the teachers for not finishing her lunch, and she was not allowed dessert. One day, the food was so bad I couldn't eat either. When I got back to class, the first thing I noticed was a large red juicy apple that a kid I called Mr. Could-Do-No-Wrong had brought in for the teacher. It was so shiny; I just had to have it. First back in class, I almost fell over the desk in a hurry to get at it. I grabbed it and took a large bite. Then I panicked. As I heard the other children coming into class, I quickly polished what was left and put the apple back, the mutilated part facing away from the teacher. Not a good plan, as the entire class could see the huge chunk out of it. Mr. Could-Do-No-Wrong screamed in horror, "Someone killed the teacher's apple!" We all had until four o'clock for the 'murderer' to own up. Fear gripping my heart and apple still stuck between my teeth, I called out, "Whoever did it should own up because the rest of us didn't." I felt if I was brave enough to say that, they couldn't possibly think I was guilty. It was a good plan! The teacher let me and Mr. Could-Do-No-Wrong go home. All the others had to stay behind after school. I should have felt guilty, and I guess I did a little. But oh, did I feel smart. Not feeling that way too often, I thought that was rather clever of me. Oh, how I longed to feel that way about my school work. If only I was good in just one subject. I hated being stupid; it was so ugly, like me.

On another occasion, Sylvia was blamed for breaking a sink, but because she insisted on her innocence, the head mistress punished the whole class by giving us the cane on the back of our hands. As painful as that was, it wasn't as hurtful as the reward system they had in school. Only those who did well academically were rewarded and treated special. And for the students whose parents had money to send for various types of funding, the reward was even greater. I had come to realize very early that I was different from others, and there was no value in me. I didn't like feeling stupid, and it wasn't true that I was lazy. I tried. I tried really hard, but I just didn't understand what the teacher meant. And I didn't feel it was my fault because my mother couldn't afford to send money. So why did I feel so ashamed, so guilty?

As Mother was expecting another child, Sylvia, Bobby, Billy and I were to be sent away. This would be the second time we were sent to an orphanage home called Warren Farm. It reminded

me of some old building from the eighteenth
century, large and tall, with small windows. The
windows looked like a thousand eyes all staring
down at me. It was so old and big, I was sure it was
haunted. It had a huge tree outside the front of the
building with long hanging, outstretched branches,
and it seemed to add to the foreboding feeling. My
sister Joan, who was only three years old, was sent to
the babies' section. My brothers were staying across
the road in the boys' compound. When Sylvia and I
first arrived, we were met by the supervisor, Miss
Salad. My first impression of her was fear. Her face
was pale, stone like, as though her face might crack
if she smiled; she had dark hair and eyes and wore
thick dark red lipstick and a white, starched coat.
She was overweight and seemed to tower over
Sylvia and me. Miss Salad had given us something
to eat. Poor Sylvia licked her knife. And with the
knife still in her mouth, Miss Salad's hand came hard
across her face. Her voice sounded like a man's,
deep, spitting. If I hadn't been so upset for Sylvia, I
would have laughed.

Billy and I were divided by a wire fence and forbidden to visit each other, but that never stopped us. We would try to pick a safe time to meet, even if for a few moments. Billy had only to come to the fence, but I had to cross the road. Whenever I was caught, Miss Salad would beat me. I sensed she enjoyed doing it; she always had a smile for me then. Sylvia and I always looked for Billy, hoping he'd be out to play at the same time as we were. Sometimes Sylvia would cross the road with me; other times she was too afraid. Sylvia was sick quite often and spent a lot of time in the infirmary. Once I missed her so much, I pretended I was sick too. It worked, and I ended up in her ward. The infirmary always looked and smelled fresh. It was much brighter than the orphanage, and it didn't have that terrible smell of carbolic soap. The walls were cream and green. There were flowers out in the front garden. When the nurses opened the doors, which they often did, I could smell the scent of lavender. The nurses were very kind to us, and I didn't want to leave. Best of all, being in the infirmary worked out well for Billy and me because my window faced the back of the field where Billy played. He would come over every day and put his head just inside the window and talk to us. One day he came to the infirmary to give Sylvia a doll that a nun had helped him make. It made me happy too because it wasn't often I saw a smile on her face any more. She had taken to biting her nails, sometimes so badly they would bleed. If she got caught, she'd get slapped.

Shortly after Sylvia and I left the infirmary, one of the girls claimed the doll was hers. Miss Salad herself came and took the doll away from Sylvia, who was so frail and frightened that just watching her sobbing tore a piece of my heart away. I went quiet and the tears did not come, as they often didn't. Taking a chance, I ran across the road looking for Billy, knowing one of the nuns in Billy's compound had helped make the doll. I thought she'd explain things to Miss Salad. If I had known the consequences, I would never have done it. Billy came over. But Miss Salad was not going to listen to a child, and she gave him an awful slap across the face. She claimed it was for lying and crossing the road without permission. Billy, his head hung low, put his hand to his face, turned and walked away.

I knew he wanted to run, but to Billy that would have been a sign of cowardice. Sylvia stood holding tightly to my arm as we watched him leave. He wasn't gone long when he returned with the nun at his side. As the nun approached Miss Salad, who was still standing in the yard, a great confrontation began. All the girls started to gather around trying to hear what was being said. Then the most unexpected thing happened. The nun slapped Miss Salad's face. Then she grabbed the doll out of her hand and yelled something about her being a godless woman. The nun took Billy's arm and walked away. Miss Salad turned around looking directly at me. She had horns, pointed ears, long teeth and was breathing fire. The flames seemed to burn my face as she came toward me. All the girls stepped back but Sylvia. As she grabbed my arm and started dragging me toward the building, my body went stiff and my feet felt like lead. I felt sick to my stomach. Sylvia was holding on so tightly to my dress it ripped as I was dragged away, and her loud sobbing sounded like she thought it would be the last we'd ever see of each other. As I was shoved through the door, my breathing was all I could hear, as though God had turned the sound off. Miss Salad pulled me up stairs, opened the linen closet door and threw me inside. She stepped in and locked the door behind her. Taking a hairbrush from her pocket, she began to beat me. Covering my body with my arms, I tried crawling under one of the shelves. However, she pulled me back by my hair, and, when I urinated, she beat me some more.

I was not alone in being tormented in this place. Because the boys' housing was overcrowded, two young boys shared a small room next to our dormitory. Both of them, as well as I, wet the bed. Each morning Miss Salad would take us down to the bathrooms, which consisted of eight bathtubs. It always stank of carbolic soap. She'd beat me first. Sometimes I'd catch a glimpse of the boys' terrified faces as they stood in their bare feet and wet pajamas. We weren't allowed to get dressed before our beating because we might wet ourselves, and it would mean more washing with our sheets. The little boy, who was no more than six or seven, would hide behind the older boy who was more my age.

I found out later both Billy and Bobby suffered over wet beds too, but in a very different manner than me. Bobby wet the bed, but because he was so young they punished Billy instead. Putting the sheets into a bathtub full of soapy water, they made Bobby watch while Billy walked up and down on them until they were clean. This did not cure Bobby, but I felt it must have filled him full of guilt and shame.

We did attend school while at the orphanage, and Sylvia was in my class, along with quite a few other 'orphans'. And none, of the other children played with us. The whispers were that their mothers didn't want them near us because no one knew where we came from. I thought we all came out of our mothers' tummies. I remember staring at the floor for most of the lessons. The wooden floor was old and dirty, and I'd watch the bugs come up in between the cracks. Watching them helped pass the time. Also, if I held my head low enough, the teacher wouldn't ask me questions, forcing me to reveal myself as a dunce.

We were only visited one time during our six months at Warren Farm. Aunty Rose seemed to have taken us under her wing, and my lasting impression of her was that she always tried to protect us. After she left that day, Sylvia became angry and frustrated. I think she thought Aunt Rose had come to take us home. A few days later, to everyone's surprise and my delight, Sylvia and another girl ran away. I was so proud of Sylvia but also in dreadful fear of the beating she would get. I prayed to Our Lady she would make it home. The thought of her being beaten never allowed me to think how much I'd miss her. Needless to say, they were brought back the same day. I thought it was strange they weren't punished and nothing was ever said. The following day after Sylvia's great escape, we and some of the girls sat outside singing on a low brick wall, which fenced off the garden. I saw something in Sylvia's face I had never seen before, a sense of pride. She knew it had taken courage to run away. The song we were singing was called "I Bought A Penny Banana." A silly title and an even sillier song, but we had fun singing it. Even the boys knew that song.

After six months, we returned home and to a new brother named Anthony, who was born October 5, 1950. He was my father's pride and joy. And I was a mistake. I knew God was mad at me because I was a very bad child. What with being a dunce, wetting the bed and breaking the rules to see my brother, no wonder they couldn't love me. I felt like a child with no soul. In a sense, if anything made sense, it was good to see my father was able to love one of us. I often thought he loved my sister Ann, but even they had their differences. However, I was always very sure he loved my mother dearly. Perhaps because there were so many of us, there just wasn't enough love to go around. At least now, when things got too bad, I had the fields and the woods to run off to.

CHAPTER 2

Toffee With Mustard Gas

Some happy moments, which I locked away in my treasure trove of memories, are of my father standing over the stove making toffee, usually on a Saturday night. I was really proud my father could cook because I thought only women knew how. One night, while making toffee, he told us kids to go into the living room and sit by the fireplace. He said once the toffee was made, he would come and tell us a true story about a haunted house that my mother and he had once lived in. My mother, preparing a big pot of tea, nearly dropped her lovely flowered china teapot and a shocked look came over her face. She said in a shaky voice, "You said you'd never talk about that and told me I was never to ask what really happened that terrible night." Dad ignored Mum, as though he hadn't heard her, and kept stirring the thick delicious toffee that I could already taste. We could barely contain ourselves. To pass the time while waiting for Dad to finish making the toffee, we listened to Dick Barton on the wireless. Dick Barton was a nightly half-hour children's program. He was a special agent, who got into all sorts of difficulties, and was always exciting to listen to. Billy put more coal on the fire. Dad came in and sat down in his favorite chair, which he seemed to sink into. It was made of a thick, red material with a flowered pattern through out and had huge armrests. It was part of a three-piece matching set that included Mum's chair and the large settee, opposite the fireplace. Mum placed a tray full of cups and saucers and a large pot of tea on the table and sat in her chair, facing Dad, each sitting on either side of the fireplace. Dad and Mum both had their favorite chairs and no one else was allowed to sit in them. Dad started to cut the toffee into small pieces. Mum turned out the lights, leaving only the glow from the coal. As Dad started talking, we all huddled closer together, and I noticed Mother pull her chair closer toward the fire. "World War II had just begun, and I was at sea serving on the H.M.S.

Arrow in the Atlantic, on patrol. Your mum had moved into a house and because I was at sea I hadn't seen it yet.   The first I heard that any thing was wrong was when I was told to go and see one of the officers aboard ship. He then informed me that I was being sent home because your mother was very sick. I was sure your mum must have been dying because no one was sent home during the war unless it was urgent. Can you imagine how angry I was when I arrived home and your mother tells me I had to come back because the house was haunted, and even more furious when I found out that you were involved too Ann?" Dad sat still, staring at Ann. I thought to myself, *Yes, I can imagine how angry you were, dad*. I felt sorry for Mum, especially since I knew Dad didn't believe in such nonsense. My sister Ann remained quiet. Dad went on. "Your mother claimed she and your grandmother and your mum's sister aunty Nell, all experienced something evil, as they put it, in the house late at night. Things were so bad; Grandma and Aunty Nell were taking turns staying with your mum because she wouldn't

stay by herself.   "Well, later that night the three of
them went on to tell me - and all at the same time -
that the first thing that happened was one morning
your mum came down the stairs to find the front
door wide open.   At first she thought she hadn't
closed it properly, even though she could have
sworn she'd locked it.   In the middle of the night,
they would often hear what sounded like someone
running up the stairs and stopping as they got to the
top of the landing."   "I could hardly breathe," Mum
said; "I thought my bedroom door was going to
burst open and as for your sister Ann!" Mum didn't
say anymore. I think it was due to Dad's look as if to
say, who's telling this bloody story.   "As your
mother said, Ann also experienced strange things at
night, but she wasn't afraid. She'd come down to
breakfast in the morning and talk about a beautiful,
big dog that came to visit her nightly. At first it was
put down to Ann's imagination; however, your
mother started to hear Ann late in the night talking
to someone. One night she opened Ann's door, and
Ann was upset because she said Mum frightened the

dog away." "Well, I was so angry that Ann had been involved in this ridiculous story, I said, that's it! I'm sleeping in Ann's bedroom just to prove you all wrong! Your Grandma and Aunty Nell were not impressed with me, and both left in a huff and in a hurry. That same night, as I slept in Ann's room, I was awakened by the sound of someone running up the stairs and knocking loudly on my door. I thought it was your mother coming to apologize for making such a fuss earlier in the day; when I saw the door handle turn slowly, I expected your mother to be standing there." Dad glanced at Mum as she moved toward the edge of her seat. Dad's voice lowered to a whisper. "But when the door opened wide, there wasn't a soul in sight. Not until I heard the sound of footsteps approaching my bed did I feel the hairs on the back of my neck stand up. Then seeing an indentation appearing on my bed as though someone had sat down, I became very afraid." Dad! Afraid?! I didn't know he could be afraid of anything. And admit it too. But I kept my thoughts to myself as I slid off the couch closer to the fire; my brothers and sisters following suit. Dad continued the story.

"A strong odor had accompanied the footsteps into the room, and I recognized the smell as traditional seamen's pipe tobacco."

Did Dad have to puff on his pipe as he said that? Trying to move closer to the fireplace was useless since by now Bobby was practically sitting in my lap with his hand covering his face as though the smoke from Dad's pipe was about to take some evil form. I wasn't sorry Dad was coming to the end of the story.

"When your Mother awoke the next day, she found me moving all the furniture out into the street. However, much later, unbeknownst to your mother, I made some inquiries about the previous tenant. I learned that an old retired fisherman had been found dead in the very room I'd slept in. He had hung himself. I didn't tell your mother because I also found out the fisherman owned a Saint Bernard dog, like the one Ann had seen so many times. Personally, I think Dad had to get over the shock himself. As I looked at Mother to see her response to the story, I would have giggled if I dared. Her mouth was wide open, as though she was trying to say something but nothing came to mind. Dad looked at Mum and said, "Once the kids have gone to bed, we'll talk some more."

Thank goodness for that, I said to myself: I don't want to hear anything else.

Mum got out of her chair, made us a cup of cocoa, asked us to kiss her good night and go to bed. We all made one mad dash toward her. Mother laughed, thinking she was unusually popular, but I knew better. No one wanted to be the last one up the stairs after that story! However, Billy seemed to think because he was a male he should go after everyone else. Heaven forbid he should show any fear! Bobby being the last had just reached the top of the stairs when Billy broke the world's record. I swear it took him all of two seconds to climb fifteen stairs.

There were happy times at Christmas too, before I reached my teen years. Dad made a big deal out of it with traditions he inherited from his mother. The birth of Christ had been very important to both my grandmas. Dad would organize games on the evening of Christmas day, and we would have a lot of fun. Although Dad would drink at Christmas, he only got tipsy. I admired that because even though Dad didn't drink that often, when he did, he usually got drunk and mean. There was no hiding from him when he got sloshed. He was always violent and somebody always got hurt. We always ran upstairs and hid under our beds. We'd wait for it to be quiet for some time before creeping down the stairs, often to finding broken furniture. I hated New Year's Eve. It reminded me of the war when we would run for cover. If Hitler dropped mustard gas, we had masks to cover our faces. With Dad, we had to use our hands.

CHAPTER 3

But The Living Of Each Year

We was leaving Ashurst Road to move into a larger house. I was heartbroken those few happy times at Ashurst Road were to be no more. We would no longer be close to the fields, ponds and woods I loved to run off to. Whatever happiness I had found at Ashurst Road, I would need to grasp onto and lock away in my small brain, into my treasure trove of memories. Aunty Rose moved to a place of her own to be closer to work. She had been very kind to us, and we missed her a lot. When we had done something wrong and we were sent to bed with nothing to eat, she sneaked sugar sandwiches up the stairs to us. My most precious memory of her was getting me out of bed every night before she retired so that I wouldn't get into trouble for wetting the bed. It rarely worked because I still often wet the bed but she never gave up trying. Aunty Rose was one of those people who lived a very quiet life; hardly anyone knew she existed. Of course she was really our great-aunty since she was Granny's sister. I didn't even know Granny had a sister until after she died and Aunt Rose moved in. Aunt Rose never married; the man she was engaged to was killed in the Boer War, and she never got over the loss. When she died, she died alone. Her only friend found her dead in her flat. I'll always remember her long black hair that never went grey, rolled up in a bun at the back of her head. If Aunty Rose died thinking she hadn't left a mark in this world, she'd be quite wrong. I would never forget Aunty Rose, and I hoped when she went to heaven the man she loved was there to meet her. My first recollection of our new home on Appledore Road was like so many others; another bad memory to add to the monster Miss Salad.

Senior school had become a safe haven for me because we had different teachers for each subject and one of the teachers was kind to me and cared about my understanding what she was teaching.

Also, I made some friends, which at thirteen, hadn't happened to me before. I think it was because the school had A, B, C, and D classes, and I was in a D class. I was with others like me who had a hard time to learn, and it made me feel comfortable. So when my parents wanted me to stay home to help them with the move, I refused. Of course it wasn't quite that simple. Two of my friends came to call on me. I think they were curious to see my new house. Margaret, who was in my class called on me with another friend to walk to school together. When they knocked at the door for me, I ran to grab my coat, hoping I could dodge my parents. My father was so enraged that I preferred school to helping my parents; he picked up a rocking horse from the kitchen and threw it at me. It missed me, but the humiliation of my friends seeing what took place felt like it had hit me anyway. I had had another incident before when Margaret had called on me. I had wet the bed, and my father told her "she has to wash her pissy sheets before she can go to school." No one talked to me for a week. Now, I would have to put up with the whisperings and strange stares again. But Brian was the only one who commented. Jokingly, he said: "I thought it was Princess Elizabeth they crowned, not Princess Ellen." He called me a princess! It almost compensated for my embarrassment during the week of that incident; Miss Corduroy came and sat next to me. She spoke to me for a while; something teachers rarely did back then. She said my spelling was improving, and she was very pleased with me. She never questioned me about anything, but she did add, "Ellen, I know you try very hard, and in my class that's all I ask of my pupils." With that she smiled, saying that she also thought I was a very well behaved student. She didn't know I was too scared of my father to be anything else. Or did she guess?

My first real nightmare took place in the new house. I had a bad dream once before, during the war. It was something to do with skeletons jumping out of the closet at me, but this one was far worse. I was fully awake lying in bed: my sister Ann in the bed next to mine. Across the room, I saw a witch playing a piano. She had her back to me, and I was filled with terror. How could this be happening? Even in the dream, I knew witches weren't real. But I could see her and everything in the room, where I had laid my clothes and left my satchel. I could even see Ann fast asleep with her back to me. My greatest fear was that the witch would turn around and stare at me. I tried to move, but nothing happened. My body was paralysed. Then what I dreaded most occurred. Screaming with laughter, the witch spun her head around and stared at me. Her face, lips and eyes were green. On her nose was a huge wart. Her teeth were filthy. She wore a tall black pointed hat over her black hair. The rest of her was black. I felt myself screaming until my throat hurt, but no one came to help me. Why couldn't anyone hear my screams? What was happening to me? The following morning, I asked Ann if she had heard any noises the night before. She said, "No, but I nearly froze to death."

Dad had opened the window as usual while

we were sleeping. I'm sure he thought he was still aboard his ship. A fanatic about fresh air, he made a habit of opening our bedroom windows before he went to bed. It was strange -considering he had suffered terribly from the cold when he had served aboard the Russian convoys during the war. Dad's shipmates had found him frozen to the controls of the guns. They had to pour warm water over his gloves in order to free him. Once I even heard Dad's best friend Percy talking about Dad being frozen, with icicles on his beard.

Several months later, I was standing at the kitchen window peeling potatoes. Dad was due home for his dinner in about an hour. Mum was in the back garden, and I could hear her giving Sylvia and Joan a telling-off because they had hung the washing on the line all wrong. My mind wandered. Ann had left school at fifteen and gone to live with Aunty Nell because of the fights between her and dad. Billy had left school at fourteen and disappeared. We thought he had joined a circus. The police were looking for him. I wondered what would happen to me when I was older. Would someone want to marry me? I thought not. One had to be pretty even to be asked out on a date. Maybe someone as plain as I or even plainer might ask me to marry him. I know I'm not ugly because I overheard my older relatives saying Sylvia was the ugly duckling of the family. I thought it strange they should say that, because to me she had an angelic face, smooth and shiny, with an air of innocence.

My thoughts returned to Bobby, Joan and Anthony who were still in school. Sylvia and I both attended Stanmer School. I was nearly fourteen and would soon be working in a factory.

God, I am so afraid! My writing is so poor and my spelling even worse. And my math, I can hardly spell the word. I could read a bit, and there were a few things I'd read to the class when Miss Corduroy asked me. My mind flashed back to thinking: What if no one does want to marry me? What will become of me? I wanted to remember this moment. I'm not sure why! Maybe, just maybe, one day I'll be peeling potatoes for my own family. Oh, I hope so!

A neighbor's voice outside broke into my thoughts. Oh, how embarrassing: she was telling Mum off because she couldn't stand her constant nagging at Sylvia and Joan.

"Can't you leave those poor buggers alone for five minutes? You're always at those poor kids. If you're not driving them crazy, you're certainly driving me nuts having to listen to you day in and day out!"

Mother didn't answer but made a quick dash into the house with Sylvia and Joan trailing behind her. I would have laughed, if part of me hadn't felt so sorry for Mother. She considered herself a real lady, always well dressed and her hair always in place. She had a way about her that could convince anyone of anything. But, as the expression goes, butter wouldn't melt in her mouth. What was even more humiliating to Mother was that the woman who had yelled at her had a husband as well as a son in prison. That's what made it funny to me; Mum being told off by someone she considered of 'lower standing'. However, the neighbor was always kind to me. If her children got into trouble, she always stuck up for them. I admired her for that.

Mother, however, did nag us a lot and, in fact, only stopped when she was watching television. Unfortunately, that didn't go on until the evening. Television was new in our house, and we only bought it because Granddad died and left money to my mother for that purpose, to buy a television. He was the one who left Grandma (Annie) with seven children for another woman.

My sister Ann went to church every Sunday without missing. I don't know where she got her faith from, but then she was the oldest and the smartest. She was even the beauty in the house. Many people said she looked just like Elizabeth Taylor. My parents seemed to love Ann. But then, she wasn't a mistake; my parents had wanted to have her. That's probably why she went to church every Sunday because God loved her. I was sure Our Lady did because Ann was devoted to her. She even had a big statue of her in her bedroom.

Mother's purpose with God was to use Him as a weapon against us. She always said the first commandment was to honor your mother and father. I always thought it was not to kill anyone. If mother was right, then I was condemned to hell because I knew I did not honor my parents, but then I didn't really know what honor meant. All I understood was that I was very unhappy and wanted to leave home. Mother seemed to be working more and more and was rarely home on the weekends, and I was quite happy about that. Poor Mum and I just did not get along at all, perhaps because we were too alike. We both seemed to go around being miserable, although Mother seemed to have stronger mood swings than I did. I was more consistent. As I grew into my teens, she seemed to get angrier with me. So I was glad when my cousin Mary, came to live with us. Since coming into her teens, she didn't get along with her mother. Billy had run off with a circus because he didn't get along with my father, Ann lived with my Aunty Nell because she didn't get along with my dad either. I wanted to leave home so badly. At least with Mary in the house, I managed to give up my imaginary friend, Jimmy, who had kept me company since we first moved to Appledore Road. I would be quite outspoken about my friend Jimmy, but only with my brothers and sisters. Outside of them, I kept Jimmy a secret. I was afraid if someone found out about him they would make fun of me, and then I'd lose him. Mary and I got along very well, and she and my sister Ann were best friends.

One night when Mary and Ann had gone to the pictures together and Mother was at work, all hell broke loose. The police brought Billy home, back from the circus. Dad took him upstairs and beat him with his belt for running away. Billy was screaming and Bobby, Joan, Sylvia and I were all standing at the bottom of the stairs crying. Sylvia and Bobby were begging Dad to stop. Anthony sat quietly in the chair where Dad had left him. The next thing we knew, Mum came running in the door from work wanting to know what was going on. It was one of those rare moments I was glad to see Mum home. With that, Dad stopped and came down the stairs. She gave him a good telling-off because she said she could hear the screaming way up the road, and the neighbors were all listening and it was embarrassing. That started a fight between Mum and Dad. Then we all got into trouble, and that was the night Dad pushed Sylvia's head into the bureau. Sylvia didn't cry until Father left the room because she said she wouldn't give him that satisfaction. When he did leave, she cried for a long time.

None of us ever held each other, and I wondered why. I loved Sylvia so much. But I stood there motionless, staring at her as though I were in a trance waiting for someone to snap his fingers and wake me up. I don't think I knew that I could hold her if I wanted to. But then, Mother never, ever hugged me that I could remember. Not ever! The following day, Mother said she'd had enough. She couldn't take anymore. She was going to kill herself. Mum was always going to kill herself because we were bad. The other threat was she would kill one of us, and they would hang her for it and it would be our fault. This day was different. She took the lid off a bottle of aspirins and emptied the entire bottle in her mouth and swallowed them. At least that's what I thought I saw. Then she went directly to bed. So, there we all were, cleaning up the house, while Father sat down in silence, and I was thinking Mum was dying. I was waiting for Dad to do something. What, I didn't know, but something! The whole scenario was insane. We were cleaning house, and Mother lay dying upstairs. Perhaps I did have some feelings after all because when Mother came down the stairs a few hours later, I was very relieved. It never occurred to me that she might spit them out in the toilet upstairs. When she came down, she went straight to the medicine cabinet and took some medication. While she did that, she told us we'd be the death of her.

Mother took a lot of medication. We would even joke about it. My brothers, sisters and I would often say, if we sold all of mother's medicine, we would be rich. I was too young to realize the serious implications of doctors prescribing so many pills for my mother. They all seemed to have the same answer for her. She'd given birth to a lot of children; she worked so hard, she needed pills to keep her going. The doctors also said we weren't helping her enough. At least that's what Mother said the doctor said. I didn't know how to help Mother any more than I was. If the truth were known, I'd given up trying. Much like my schooling, I just didn't do things right. Sylvia would slave away to please Mother. It never worked, but she never gave up. Watching Sylvia made me feel even worse about myself. I liked trying to please Dad who seemed more receptive, but I rarely got the chance. One time though I did. Mother had gotten Dad to write a letter to the school because she was suspicious that Bobby and Joan were spending their canteen money on candy. When Mum didn't receive an answer and questioned Joan and Bobby, they said the teacher hadn't had time to write back yet. Somehow I just knew that was a lie. I knew the teacher had never received the letter. Bobby and Joan had ripped it up, and I knew where they had thrown it. I wanted my father's approval so desperately that I went to the field and found all the pieces. When I showed Dad the torn letter to prove to him I was a good girl, worthy of his love, he did the strangest thing. He stared at me for what seemed forever. A look I didn't understand. Then he asked me if I wanted to help him in the shed that afternoon. Of course, I was thrilled because that was what we all strived for. If one of us were chosen to help Dad in the shed, that made us feel special. He never did beat Bobby or Joan. Even odder, he asked me not to mention it to Mother. Later that night, I asked myself what would have happened if Dad had beaten Joan and Bobby. How would I have felt? I had betrayed those I loved most. Thank goodness Dad had taken the attitude he did. If only he would have told me what he was thinking, but then Dad never did.

Time passed and the day came when I was to leave school. I was fourteen. I had finally stopped wetting the bed and that made me realize my body was changing. Why stopping wetting the bed made me realize that, I don't know. I was considered tall for a girl, very plain to look at and skinny.

My mother was always cutting my hair short, and at that time the latest fashion in hairstyles was the Basin Cut. But she took that literally and stuck one of those old type, yellow bowls on my head, took the scissors and cut around it. Blimey! It was a mess. But, that's how I graduated - fourteen, a bowl hair cut and illiterate.

My first job was at a factory called Harrimonds, where they made dresses. I can't say I was looking forward to work because I had no idea what to expect. However, I learned quickly to keep my mouth shut: Although that wasn't hard for me to do. There were always fights between the girls over something, usually over a bloke. What was most humiliating to me was that while working there I learned nothing. For three months they tried training me to use a sewing machine. Finally, they gave up. They sat me with the older women to cut off the cotton ends of the dresses that were left from sewing them on the machines.

It was bad enough being scared to go to work, but then there was also the humiliation of having to take jam sandwiches every day for lunch. There just never seemed to be anything else in the pantry, and, if there was, it was always locked up. I never bought a cup of coffee or tea at work because I never had any money. Not making much money to start with, I had to give it all to mother for my keep. My first pay cheque was around two pounds, two shillings, three pence and half a penny. In Canadian dollars, that would have been about six dollars. What little mother gave me back wasn't even enough for my bus fare to work. I had to walk to work everyday. It wasn't just that it was over two miles away, I was used to walking everywhere. It was the man with the red curly hair who would chase my friend Margaret and me across the fields every morning. He would hide in the bushes and wait for us. We never knew quite where he would be, so we would start to run the moment we got close to the bushes.

His hair stuck out all over the place. His face matched the colour of his hair, red with anger. His eyes were squinty. Almost every morning, he would jump out at us, bellowing as he chased us. One time I thought he was going to catch Margaret. She was so frightened she started to cry and could hardly run anymore. We both started to scream, and he seemed to enjoy that and stopped chasing us. Margaret was terrified and complained to the police, but they told her since he never actually touched us they thought he was harmless. There was no other route to take unless we took the long route, about five miles. At any rate, Margaret and I never let him catch us. Being frightened of work itself was one thing. But being harassed on the way there by a crazy man was too much. I quit my job. Long after that, I heard from different sources that the man's name was Mr. Walker. He had five children, and he slept with his daughters. My mind could not conceive of such an act. When it came to sex, my emotions were in serious trouble. The red-headed man had awakened a memory in me, taking me back to when I was four.

The police did not find the man from that incident, and told my mother that I'd never remember if no one talked about it. So I hated the redheaded man Mr. Walker because he awakened a memory that my teenage years could not handle. I knew sex was a very bad thing because of all the fuss that the police had made so many years ago. And I remember my mother putting me in the bath so I would be clean again. But the dreadful memory and shame remained. I'd have nightmares that Mr. Walker was stabbing me. There was blood everywhere. I wished I'd hurry up and die in the dream, but he just kept stabbing me. I'd wake up crying, and the loneliness and fear I felt would last all day. Sometimes is lasted longer, turning to depression. If all this meant I was now grown up, I hated it.

After leaving the dress factory, I took a job working in a hotel. I started my period while working there. Truly, I had no idea what was happening to me. My first thought was to go to the hospital. But since I was losing blood from such a personal place, I was too embarrassed and decided not to.   When I got home later that evening and since I was still bleeding, I told Sylvia. Fortunately, she had her period already and told me all about it. She wasn't quite sure why we had to have it, but she had heard from her friends that if it suddenly didn't come anymore, it meant that you were going to have a baby. That's when I asked Sylvia:

"What happens if it stops and you're not married yet?"

"Well if you're not married it won't happen."

"But Sylvia, how will it know when to stop, just because you get married?"

"I don't know I just heard that in the washroom at school. Maybe it's not even true. All I know is you get it once a month and you will have to buy some sanitary pads."

"Blimey. What do you mean sanitary pads?"

"You have to go to the chemist and ask for a box of sanitary pads."

"Are you crackers, Sylvia? Are you totally nuts? Men work as chemists. I'm not going to embarrass myself and ask for those things, whatever you call them!"

"Sod you then Ellen, bleed to death! See if I care!"

What does it mean to be a woman? What does it mean to me? But I was too upset to think about it right then. That week I was sacked from my job at the hotel. They said I was too slow. I didn't understand. I worked so hard polishing all the furniture. I was late some mornings, but I did explain to the boss that I caught the first bus downtown, and I couldn't get there before then. This meant I'd have to find another job, probably in a factory. I knew they were always desperate for workers and would take anyone, even me.

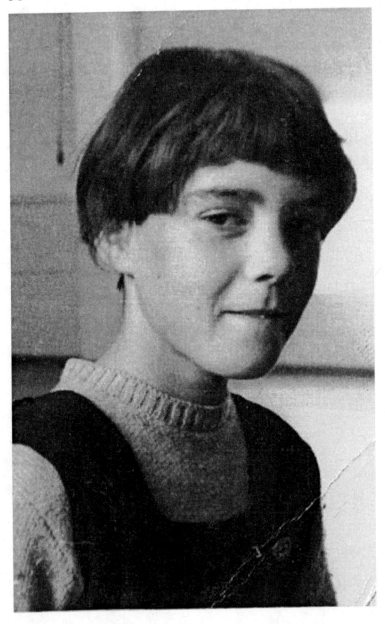

CHAPTER 4

Crying In the Rain

D ad was dying of cancer, and once again we were on the move. I knew nothing about death. I had thought about it a great deal, but only in regard to my own death, certainly not Father's. As my cousin Mary and I packed our clothes into boxes and listened to the rain pouring down our bedroom window, I wondered why we should move because Dad was dying. But no one was allowed to discuss his illness because it might upset him. We had to keep it a secret from Dad, who already knew he was dying! Dad refused to leave work. He had started working at Hollingbury only a short time ago, and was really enjoying it. Even when suffering the most severe pain, he would take his bike and ride to the factory a couple of miles away. Cancer was not new to our family; Granny had died from stomach cancer. Mother nursed Dad with tremendous gentleness. She could never do enough for him. She got a lot of sympathy, and that gave her even more energy to take care of him. But she used Father's illness to get her own way about everything. That made the bitterness between us even more unbearable.

What did I feel about Dad dying? Nothing! Was it even true? Mother exaggerated so much, I really couldn't be sure. Dad was very sick and had a lot of surgery, but dying? Once when we lived at Ashurst Road, Dad had been sick and we talked about him dying then. My brothers and sisters and I were in the toy room and we all agreed that if one of our parents had to die, it should be Dad because he hit us harder than Mum. Years later Sylvia confessed to me, she used to pray that Dad would die. Then she became afraid God would punish her for her thoughts. Often when Dad arrived home from work, he was all out of breath, but he never complained and always brought home a chocolate bar for Anthony. Joan wasn't much older than Anthony but he never thought to bring her anything. At least he gave her a nickname, like he did most of us. Joan was 'Bomb Happy,' Billy was 'The Black Sheep,' Sylvia was 'The Nail Biter' and I was 'Zombie.' Ann didn't have a specific nickname. Anthony, could do no wrong, and was called by his Christian name. Bobby seemed almost without any name, but he was always the one with the jokes. Bomb Happy, I later found out was a term used for people emotionally disturbed by the war, particularly service men that had experienced bombs dropping day after day.

Billy had gone to sea with the merchant navy. I was happy for him because when he did come home, everybody was pleased to see him, even Dad. Billy would never stay very long. He and Dad seemed to get along better if his visits were short I often wondered how Billy had felt about Mum and Dad putting him away. When he had run away with the circus, they had said he was out of control. The judge sent him to St. Swithin's for nineteen months. It was run by the de la Salle Brothers of the Christian Schools. Billy said they were very strict, but actually thought it had done him a lot of good.

Ann married at eighteen. I suspect marriage was a safe place for her to be. Everyone loved her husband Don. They met at work, at a factory called Allen West. Nearly everyone in Brighton must have worked there at one time or another.

Sylvia had finished school at fourteen and was working as a live-in nanny. I was now working with Mary in a factory called Dentsupply, making false teeth. I wondered what it would be like to go to a dentist. I enjoyed working with Mary, but it didn't last long; the business was not doing too well, and each week more and more people were given a week's notice. They let the women go first. That surprised me since the men were paid almost twice what the women received, and many women were doing jobs that required a lot more skill. I guess men were considered more important than women because they had to bring money in for their families. Although I wasn't let go, I knew it was inevitable, so I found another job. On my last day at work, I was given all the money due to me, including the nearly a week's wages that I had saved through the company savings club. It was more than I'd ever had in my life, and Mother knew nothing about it. I never told her anything when it came to my wages regarding raises or savings. When it came to money, Mother seemed to worry so much. There was no trust between us. I made sure my parents never saw the things I would buy, like the new shoes. Like most of my clothes, I hid them. Before going out, I'd stuff my shoes in my handbag along with my makeup and hide my Italian Skirt and shocking-pink sweater underneath my coat. Once I got off the bus at the Old Stein, I went into the lavatory and changed my clothes. I was still only fifteen and didn't date, but I would go out to some of the coffee bars and halls that had rock and roll dances. My favorite place for dancing was the Regent, and my favorite coffee bar was Whiskey A Go Go. I never did learn how to dance. I was awful at it. But I was so in love with Elvis Presley, I made myself dance to his music. I saw all his films. And strange as it may sound, Elvis gave me a reason to keep on living. I had I had collected many pictures of Elvis, but I made a stupid mistake in putting them on my bedroom wall. Dad saw them, ripped them all down and threw them in the dustbin. Ann had just happened to pay Mum and Dad a visit that night, and she came into my bedroom and found me crying. She was horrified. She retrieved the pictures from the dustbin and hid them for me. Then she sent her husband Don to get some fish and chips for everyone. She told me to go with him, knowing I loved motorbikes. So off I went sitting in the sidecar of Don's bike. That was a smashing idea, and I loved riding in it. Don and I drove all over Devil's Dyke before going to the fish and chip shop. When we got back, everyone wanted to know what had taken so long; we explained that the queue at the fish and chip shop was miles long.

Don introduced me to his friend Michael, whom I dated for a few months and would have married, but his mother didn't approve of me. My parents actually pushed me toward marriage; they thought he was such a nice boy. He was, but my main reason for wanting to marry him was that he was so handsome. I couldn't believe he'd want me. I would be married and have security, and a handsome bloke was a real bonus. Dating Michael, I became more confused about sex than ever before, and, like math at school, what I didn't understand, I disliked. My parents never discussed sex. I thought it was something to be ashamed of. The closest I ever saw my parents in the nude was once when I forgot to knock on their bedroom door and walked in to find my father in his under-shorts. He was so angry he threw a hairbrush at me, hitting the side of my face. As for mother, the most I saw of her body was when she was in her dressing gown. Catholic schools did emphasize that Mary was a blessed virgin. Remembering the experience from when I was four, I guessed sex was something really evil. Having had sex with Michael before marriage probably meant I would go to hell. How could I go to confession and tell a priest I'd had sex willingly? A friend told me priests don't have sex. Maybe if I went to confession, he wouldn't know what I was talking about. I didn't go to confession because I believed I was already condemned to hell for all the other rotten things I had done. I probably had more sins than venial ones. You only need one mortal sin to go to hell. Even if I got rid of all the mortal sins, then what happens to the venial ones? I thought maybe there were two types of hell, one hot, one boiling. I guess I'm fried!

So when my money disappeared from my handbag, I knew Mother had taken it. I took on a lot of pain that day. I had plans for my money. I know Dad knew the truth, but he often made sacrifices to keep the peace! Until that time I had thought Dad ruled the house. Well, there were a lot of mouths to feed.

Finally, I made up my mind to leave home. For a while, I lived with a family looking after their children. That didn't last long. Mother kept phoning the woman of the house, telling her how sick Dad was. The woman, not knowing Mother and her ways, said I should leave because my Mother needed me at home. My explanation about Dad, that he was still working, didn't change her mind. That was the first time I had lived in a house with a phone and I hated it: it lost me my job. After that I changed jobs many times. As long as I could sign my name and push my time card in the machine, I could work in any factory. Not being able to stand going home anymore, I ran away and stayed with a friend. That freedom was short-lived. The police came and picked me up. But they did not take me straight back home. They took me down to the police station and locked me in a room. A police-woman told me to look at the things in the glass case while they decided what to do with me. The display case was full of straps, canes, and other things that children had been beaten with. This ignorant policewoman was trying to tell me that I had no reason to run away like some children did. I kept thinking, Stupid! Stupid cow! Blimey, not only had my father beaten me with a belt, he even kept a cane on top of the door ledge for variety. I had been beaten at home, at school and at the orphanage, whether I had done wrong or not. I felt like screaming at the policewoman.

"You should see *my* glass case!! Hairbrush, straps, a cane and a blackboard brush which a teacher threw at me full force in the face because I didn't understand a math question. You should see all that"!!

But the screaming remained inside my head. I was too cowardly to speak, a gutless idiot. No one would believe me. The police came back and threatened to put me in a home for wayward girls. My reply wasn't what they expected, and they thought I was being lippy. Dear God, I wasn't! I wanted to be put away! Eventually, they put me in a police car and took me home, but not before they were ready to throttle me too. On the way home, the policewoman told me I was a stupid girl. She had spoken to my mother. She asked me how I could be so cruel in her time of need. She also made a negative comment on my clothes, even the shoes I was wearing. My thoughts trailed off to the day I bought those shoes. It had been so exciting. When I walked into the store, the first thing I noticed was a red carpet and the smell of leather. The sales clerk came up to me and asked; "Can I help you Madam?" I felt like Cinderella, and I wanted to throw my arms up in the air and yell out, "I feel so very special. I've come to buy the shoes of my choosing!!" It was my first time buying what I liked. I knew what I wanted. I'd looked at them in the window so many times. And now here I was trying them on, my very favorite Winkle Pickers! Yes, at long last they were on my feet; the most beautiful shoes I'd ever seen. They came to very long points. Sometimes I'd have to walk up narrow stairs sideways. I had planned to buy a pair with my savings, but since Mum took my money I had to save again. It took me six weeks. It gave me a wonderful feeling of independence to go into that shoe shop. We finally arrived at home at my house, and between the policewoman and Mother, I was a selfish teenager. After the police left, I had to listen to Mother for an hour: I was selfish, I had a lovely home and why would I run away? That was the first time I learned about what the Jewish people had suffered. Mother told me about the unbelievable atrocities of the holocaust: the point being that by comparison I had nothing to gripe about. Thinking about what happened to the Jewish people did make me feel very guilty that I had ever thought things were so bad. Those poor Jewish people, having whole families killed. After all that, I wondered if the Jewish people still believed in God. When I found out that for many their faith was even stronger and that hundreds had gone to Israel to start all over, I was in awe of their courage. To me they will always be special because they never gave up hope, whereas I knew mine was fading fast. Mother was most concerned as to what I might say if the neighbors questioned me about being brought home in a police car. Anything would do so long as the neighbors didn't know I'd run away from home.

There were so many songs written that were so close to my heart; Only The Lonely, That's The Way Of A Clown, Love Me Tender, Don't Be Cruel, and The Great Pretender. But my very favorite was

an old one called The Twelfth of Never.   The Everly
Brothers "Crying in the Rain" haunted me as I sat
alone in my room.

I'll never let you see the way my broken
heart is hurting me,
I've done my crying and I know how to hide
all my sorrow and pain,
And I'll do my crying in the rain.
Someday when my crying's done,
I'm going to wear a smile and walk in the sun,
I may be a fool, but until then
You'll never see me complain,
I'll do my crying in the rain.

Chapter 5

Warm August Night

It didn't seem possible for things to deteriorate more between Mother and me, but they did. I broke up with Michael. No one was more surprised than I was. I'm not sure what changed my mind. He was in the army at the time and was sent off to Cyprus. The idea was I'd wait until he came back. He'd be twenty-one and we could marry. But I didn't want to be shut in for two years waiting for him. I wanted to go to the coffee bars, go dancing, smoke cigarettes behind my parents' backs, stare at the blokes and wear my Winkle Pickers. Mum just didn't understand why I jilted him; and what was worse, neither did I! Wasn't that what I wanted! A husband and someone to take care of

me?   Wasn't security what every woman wanted?

Once again my family was on the move. This time it was to a flat because Dad was too ill to do the garden. It was February 1958, I should have been used to moving, but I hated it. As we packed our furniture into the lorry, I wondered how long it would be before Mother decided to move again.

After Michael, I didn't date much. I had begun to see myself as ugly and even uglier inside, to the point of hating myself. I was disgusted with my body. I wondered what the purpose to my life was. I failed in school, at work and at home. Dating scared me. God didn't love me. I couldn't even dance properly; I felt people were laughing at me just like they had in school. I didn't know what love really meant. Was it sex; and if so, why did it make me feel so uncomfortable? I ran away from home because I felt unwanted and unloved. Mother had said she only wanted two children. I was the beginning of Mother's errors. Ideas of suicide crept into my mind more and more often.

Billy was at sea. Ann and Don, with their baby daughter, had immigrated to Canada. Sylvia was still working as a nanny, and rarely came home. She was allowed only one day off a week. If she did come home for the day, Mother would charge her for meals, and she was only receiving a small wage. Bobby, Joan, and Anthony were still in school, and I didn't see much of them. If I was home -and I tried not to be- I'd stay in my bedroom until it was time to go to work the next day.

One evening, my friend Livia Leach, who lived just a few doors down from me, asked me to go to a dance with her. It was a Friday night, and it sounded like a smashing idea. Livia was always a lot of fun and much more outgoing than I was. She was very pretty and petite, with dark brown eyes and lovely short blonde hair. I was glad, Livia asked me out. I hated being at home. Recently Mum and Dad were getting a lot of visitors, especially family, due to Dad's illness. It was always the same story; every time some bloody member of the family came over; they wanted to know if I was helping Mother.

If I were getting ready to go out, I'd get dirty looks
and some snippy comment. Why aren't you staying
to help your Mother? Or at the very least you could
keep her company. Mother and I couldn't stand to
be in the same room with each other. Worse, I still
wasn't sure if I believed Dad was going to die. But
he did look awful. If only Dad had talked to me
about it.

That evening, we went dancing at the
Aquarium. The Aquarium was famous for its
display of fish and other animals. My favorite was
Polly, a parrot that was always outside at the top of
the steps. Livia and I went to see the animals prior
to going into the dance hall. Some sailors were there
teaching Polly to swear. Just as a couple of elderly
women went by, the sailors gave Polly great
encouragement to curse. One lady went up to the
parrot saying, 'Pretty Polly, Pretty Polly.' When the
parrot told her where to go, denoting sex and travel,
I thought she'd have heart failure; she went quite
blue. Livia and I giggled all the way into the dance
hall. I was wearing a royal blue mohair dress with

short sleeves. It went straight down to the knees, with a big buckle that came under the bust. Michael had bought it for my last birthday. It looked very good on me. Livia had done my hair in the beehive style. And of course I had on my famous beige Winkle Pickers! I felt like the cat's meow that night! I was feeling so good about myself, I forgot I didn't dance well and wore out my shoes to Elvis, Roy Orbison, Tommy Steel, Buddy Holly, The Big Bopper, Paul Anka, and Little Richard. I was supposed to be home at ten o'clock, but we were having such a good time that we missed the last bus. Now we had to walk home. As I got halfway up my street, I saw my father waiting just outside looking around for me. We lived in a block of flats on the second floor. He started to beat me at the front door, but somehow I ended up in Bobby's bedroom. At one point, I fell to the floor and tried to hide under his bed, but Bobby had already heard the ruckus from his bedroom window and had beaten me to it.

I was crying. My hair was a mess. But when I saw my blood on my blue mohair dress, I sobbed in earnest. I cupped my hand to my nose, and I noticed one of my shoes had turned up at the end. I must have bent it. Blood had dripped on both of them. I made my way to my bedroom. I could probably wipe the blood off the shoes, but how would I get the stains out of my dress? At that moment, I heard a voice from outside shouting up at my bedroom window.

"Ellen! What the bloody hell's going on? Christ almighty! The whole neighborhood can hear you being beaten." It was my friend Livia's mother.

"Ellen! Get your things and get down here right now. You're coming to sleep over at my house tonight."

My parents made a quick exit to their bedroom, and the house went deathly quiet. Mother would be dying with embarrassment listening to Mrs. Leach calling out to me. The neighbors had heard it all. Grabbing a few of my clothes, I ran down the stairs and out into the street. Mrs. Leach put her arm around me and took me back to her house. She was one of the only two neighbors who ever asked me about what was going on in the house. The rest of the neighbors just whispered to each other. She wanted to call the police that night, but I asked her not too. I was afraid it would make things worse. Always in the back of my mind was this little voice saying, "It's not that bad. There are children who have it much worse than you. And shouldn't you have been watching the time? Then you wouldn't have missed the last bus home." What perplexed me most was somehow I couldn't stand the thought of my parents getting into trouble.

The following day, waking up at Livia's house, something inside me failed. It was as though I'd been inside a well for a long time hanging on with one hand. That hand now had given way, and I had fallen to the bottom, a crumpled heap of what was left of a little girl, lost, alone, drowning. My thoughts began to race. "I can never go back home. Where can I live? How can I get my clothes out of the house without my parents seeing?"

Mrs. Leach broke into my thoughts. "Ellen! Come on in the kitchen. I've made you a nice cup of tea and a bit of breakfast."

"Thanks. I'll have the tea, but I can't eat anything."

"You get in this kitchen and get something in your stomach."

"My mum's right, Ellen," Livia said, "You have to eat."

As frightened as I was, and with nowhere to go, I went back home later that evening. All was silent. Mum had gone to work, and Dad was sitting in the living room on his own. When I walked in, his head was bent low. He looked as though he was in deep thought. He said nothing. I thought he might be in pain, but I couldn't ask. I wasn't allowed.

Going into my room, my blue dress still crumpled on the floor, I sat on my bed in the dark, thinking desperately of where I could go. Looking at the empty bed across from me where Sylvia once slept, I realized how much I missed her and Ann. Hearing a train go by, I got up and looked out of the window.

The moon was full. And I thought of love, but there was none for me. I had to get out of this house and find somewhere else to live. Then an awful question crossed my mind: If I did leave, would Mum have me brought back by the police like the last time? Oh God! What was I going to do?

I must have fallen asleep, for the next thing I remember was waking up and hearing my mother's voice in the living room. Realizing she was home from work, I grabbed my red coat and ran off down the road. For all the anguish I was feeling, I was aware it was a beautiful warm summer's evening. I walked for hours. It was August. My birthday was due, and I would be seventeen. Another year older! I don't want to grow older! People will expect things from me that I don't know how to give. I have no education. Sex frightens me, yet I desire it. But that's the problem. I don't know what I want or what I was supposed to want. Sex is the most confusing to me. No one talks about it and millions do it. Men are great at it and women are sluts, unless they're married. Then it's only done in the dark, late at night because... well. Because, what? It can't be because they don't want God to see. He knows and sees everything. That's why I'm in big trouble with Him. And by the way God, if it's so disgusting, why did you make us this way? I guess only your mother could be a virgin because she had to be very special. I'm supposed to love my parents, and it's a sin if I don't. God's mad at me for that and a whole pile of other things. Not that I blame Him for being mad at me. His son died so I might live, and I don't want to. I haven't been to church for a long time. What's even worse is everyone knows when I have my period because I'm so ill on the first day. The pain is unbearable, and it makes me vomit. To stay home means losing a day's pay and I can't afford to do that. Maybe that's why Dad is so stubborn about continuing work when he is so ill; he knows the family has to eat. I reached the ocean and could hear the waves breaking. It was my favorite place. I was unaware of the time. It must have been close to midnight, but I didn't much care. There was not a soul in sight, and my footsteps were so quiet on the pavement. Hurrying down to the beach, breaking the silence as I walked on the pebbles, I stepped right up to the water. The sky was full of stars, and left me feeling in awe and sadness. It was so beautiful, yet I was so unhappy. Seeing the pier to my right, I longed to be standing on it at the end, surrounded by my beloved ocean. Next thing I knew, I was standing at the locked gate of the pier. Making sure no one saw, I climbed over. As I walked toward the end of the pier, I noticed the rides were locked up. I wondered who would be riding on them tomorrow. I could almost hear the bumper cars banging into one another and the screams of laughter from the children riding the ghost train. I could hear the little ones calling to their mothers. I stood at the end of the pier, looking down into the ocean. I knew what my intentions were, and I had no fear. My being was calm and the rage in my heart was quiet. The waves were bobbing back and forth as though beckoning to me, waiting to catch me, to embrace me in their arms. As I stepped up on to the ledge of the wall, I wondered if the water would be cold. I hoped it would be over with quickly.

Just as I went to jump, I heard a seagull cry as though begging me not to render up my soul too soon. At that same moment, someone gently took my hand. A soft voice said, "Come down from the wall, lest you should fall."

As I stepped down slowly, clinging to the hand, numbness and fatigue came over me. I found myself staring into the face of a policeman, his eyes moist with tears.

If he spoke to me as he walked me home, I was unaware. I remember only that he kept his arm around me the whole way.

While I reached for the key from inside the letterbox, the policeman said, "Ellen, when tomorrow comes, I promise you will feel differently. God bless you and keep you safe."

Who was he? How did he know my name? Maybe it's true what the Catholic Church says: we all have a guardian angel. Whoever he was, he wasn't angry with me. If he had taken a harsh attitude toward me that night, I would have just tried to take my life again. Instead, he showed compassion and caring. He gave me a second chance at life. And he didn't report me. That would have been devastating. It's against the law to commit suicide. They can have you in hospital for forty-eight hours, and then you see the doctor who deals with crazy people. That's what they would say about me, that I was cracked. How I longed for someone to understand that the only insanity was the living of my life.

CHAPTER 6

Children of a Green Harvest

M any times during my teenage years, I felt
like a stalk of green corn, the sun never
touching my face, never allowing me to grow. I did
not know which direction to turn, or how to open up
so that the sun could warm the center of my roots
that I might turn a golden yellow.

I finally moved out of the house to share a flat
with a girl called Sheila. She was taller and eighteen
-a year older than me. For a while, I felt like a tiger
let out of a cage, and I loved it. But Sheila had run
away from an unhappy home too. Between the two
of us, living together was almost catastrophic.

Both our pay packets were menial, and many
times we went without food and electricity. This
meant we would sit in bed all evening to keep warm.
Our only salvation was my dear brother Billy, who
bailed us out a few times. Often when he was home
from sea he paid my rent, and gave me money for

the gas meter. He never turned up at the flat without food. He'd hide money under the teapot so I wouldn't find it until long after he'd gone. Many times he took Sheila and me out dancing to rock and roll, and bought us packs of Woodbines to smoke. He took us to coffee bars after dancing and bought us meals.

One night as he watched Sheila and me eat, he must have realized it was our first meal of the day. Rather than let us see the tears in his eyes, he jumped up and put three pence in the jukebox and played Paul Anka's, "Diana." He never, ever, came home from sea without a present for me. I still treasure an exquisite cigarette case he brought back from Japan; on the front was a colored picture of Mount Fiji. It was wrapped inside a lovely silk yellow scarf. He was muscular, tall, dark, very handsome and a real softy. I loved him dearly. But then he took off to South Africa.

Sheila was sacked because she had too many days off, and we ended up paying the rent out of my pay packet. Our only source of entertainment was an old record player with some records Billy had given us before leaving for South Africa. The plate wouldn't turn around on its own so for hours we would take turns spinning the plate with our fingers.

One day while Sheila was spinning the plate and we listened to the Platters' "Twilight Time," we talked about how hungry we were and where we could get some food. Somehow we got onto the subject of prostitutes and how lucky they were making all that money doing nothing but selling their bodies. Before we realized it, we were saying all we need is one night out, and we would have groceries for a week. However, we had nothing to wear that made us look the part. And besides would a bloke take us seriously, considering we were so young? That's when I had the brilliant idea of dying my hair red. How would we find money for this ingenious project? The pawnbroker! But what did we have to sell? We had sheets, Sheila's ring and some china. So off we went to sell our worldly goods to get hair dye, to have a night on the street, to be able to buy food.

"Oh Sheila, it's a brilliant red! I've got to wash it out. It's terrible. It looks like I'm bleeding to death."

"It's just for tonight. Tomorrow we'll have lots of money, and you can dye it back to its natural color. Anyway, you wanted to look like a tart. Well, now you do!"

A tart: Why did that give me an awful, sick feeling? Shame: Shame and guilt had lived with me since I could remember. I felt like a whore, but I hadn't even done anything yet.

There we were standing on West Street, notorious for prostitution. Sheila thought it would be better if we were separated. I didn't like that idea, standing on my own; someone not very nice might try to pick me up. However, she insisted, and crossed the street.

We were wearing thick makeup. I wore blue eye shadow, black pencil around my eyes, lots of red rouge and bright red lipstick. That was important, the bright red lipstick.

Perhaps if it had been summer, we may have waited a little longer, but it was winter and bitterly cold. After fifteen minutes, we went back home.

As we sat together in the double bed that night trying desperately to keep warm, we both went into shock. What would have happened to our lives if the night had gone the way we had expected? Would it have ended that one night? Had we really thought about what it would actually mean? It was too horrifying to talk about. We sat in silence for a long time. Sheila began to cry. Huddling together to keep warm we both wept for a long time.

Finally Sheila said, "Ellen, what if a man had picked you up; where would you have taken him?"

"Back to his place I guess."

"What if he was married and you couldn't go back to his place?"

"Married! Don't be ridiculous Sheila. I wouldn't go off with a married man! How could you think such an awful thing of me?"

"How much would you have charged him then?"

"I don't know; enough for a week's groceries, I think; probably two pounds, ten shillings. How much would you have charged?"

"Five pounds, I'd charge them a lot. I'd make them pay! What if an old man or a fat one tried to pick you up, Ellen?"

"What a disgusting thing to say. Never! Not on your Nelly! If he hadn't been good looking, I'd just tell him to go away. Blimey Sheila, what do you think I am, a slut?"

Sheila mumbled something about hating sex and her stepfather, and as long as he was living with her mother she'd never go back home. I wondered what she meant.

Somehow every time we seemed close to starving to death, Sheila managed to come home with groceries. When I asked her where she got the money, she said she still had the key to her house and would go home while her parents were at work and gets some food. Being the half-wit that I was, I never doubted her. But then one evening, I had just returned from work when the landlady called me down to her flat. She told me Sheila had robbed two gas meters! Apparently, when the gasman had come around to empty the meters, the bloke's next door and ours were empty. Sheila had recently gotten very chummy with the man in the next room. It didn't take much to figure out what had been going on.

We were all out on the street the next day. What a sight with our pillowcases full of all that we owned in the world.

As absurd as it sounds, I was glad to go back home. My life was going nowhere.
Thoughts of suicide had started to creep back into my mind. So when I became ill, it was with a sigh of relief.

I was ill for many weeks and the doctor came almost every day. Whatever was wrong with me was a secret. I felt like a mushroom. Kept in the dark and fed bullshit. It was regrettable they didn't grant us human beings the right to intelligence, to know what was wrong with our bodies, especially since we had to live with them day in and out. But

Mother couldn't keep anything to herself. The neighborhood and I soon learned that my heart was in trouble.

Mother was so different when someone was sick; she took wonderful care of me. Many times I wondered what went on in her mind. However, something was different this time. I'd catch mother staring at me when she thought I wasn't looking. Her face seemed to resemble a little girl's, and she seemed lost in thought. Mother asked me a couple of times if I had been eating properly. It hadn't occurred to me that I was badly underweight. Of course I said yes because I would never admit that living away from home had been a complete failure.

One morning, I caught her looking at me through the mirror, unaware I could see her. Her eyes were full of tears. The following day she went out and bought me the most beautiful white sweater. I was surprised, but happy she did that for me.

It was around that time that Buddy Holly was killed, and I couldn't understand why a person who was so talented and had so much to offer would die.

He brought so much joy to people's lives, and here I was, a nothing, and still alive.

CHAPTER 7

H.M.S. Ivernia

While I was ill, Dad stayed home with me instead of going to work. He had never done that for me before. One day he even put his arms around me and said he was worried about how thin I was. I wondered why it took a crisis for Dad, who was so ill, to put his arms around me now. I wanted to comfort him too, but I didn't know how. It was all too late.

Someone had bought Dad a rosary, and I often found him asleep in his chair, his rosary hanging from his hand. Watching him, I wondered: "Who is he, this man sitting in a chair dying before my very eyes, holding on to a chance for life after death? What did he think or feel? What had he wanted out of life? What was his favorite color? Who was this man I had lived with for eighteen years? Who, indeed, was this man whom I had called Father?"

Ann was coming home for Christmas, after having lived in Canada for two years. She now had three children; seven-month-old twins, a boy and a girl, and her oldest child Deborah. Don was working up north, so she took the opportunity to visit Dad. He had lost a lot of weight and at times was incoherent. Two weeks before Ann arrived, Father collapsed as he biked to work. His workmates found him lying on the road and brought him home. I don't remember him ever going outside the house again after that. He had begun to look like someone out of Belsen Concentration Camp.

Dad was thrilled with Ann's children, and I was glad he could see them before he died. Although I realized dad was dying, I could not accept that it was imminent. He could die in ten years or later, but not now. I was torn. If he died, it might be a monkey off my back. Yet there was also fear. Who would think, feel, speak or make decisions for me? Once father died, I would have to control my own life, and I did not know how. Perhaps I should have married Michael...

We got through Christmas, but I remember very little of that day. For some reason, my mind wandered back to the month of June, when Mum and Dad had taken a holiday to Cornwall. It was the only holiday they ever had in their entire lives. I wondered why? Was it because they could never afford it before? But then, neither could they in June.

I felt as though the world was insane. The war to end all wars didn't accomplish its goal. Mother and Father were going to travel when Dad retired, but that wasn't to be. I wanted to write a book, but doubted I would ever accomplish my goal, since I was a dunce, barely able to write my own name. My heart ached to write. As I pushed it from my mind, I wondered how many people had dreams like mine to be smashed and crushed, like the dreams of so many young who were killed in wars. However, we are here thinking, seeing, crying, laughing, feeling all the pain and wondering if the word 'joy' is some sort of a joke. Perhaps happiness is only for those who were special, or maybe just for the rich?

So when Ann asked me to go back to Canada with her, it seemed like a miracle, an escape from all the pain and confusion, a brand new life, leaving behind all the sickness.

I was fifteen when Ann first went to Canada, and I had tried to emigrate then, but they had laughed at me. The immigration department even told me I would have to go back to school. I wandered why Canada was so backward that teenagers had to stay in school three years longer that the British. However, time allowed me to emigrate and even loaned me the money for the fare. Friends warned that there would be snow most of the year and that the country was mostly wilderness. They said the trees were very tall and natives lived there; in fact, they had been there long before white men first arrived. I'd only ever seen Indians in movies and wondered if they were friendly now.

Needing pocket money for my trip, I applied for a tax rebate and received fifteen pounds, which was equivalent to roughly forty Canadian dollars. That was the most money I'd ever had in my life. I could purchase my passport, and it would get me through at least four months, six if I was really careful.

The weeks seemed to pass slowly to the sailing date. It was agonizing because there was so much tension in the house. One night Mother started hitting me and put her hands around my throat. Ann had to pull my mother off. Of course I ran to my place of refuge, Mrs. Leach's house. She made me stay there that night and put ointment on the marks where my mother's hands had pressed on my throat. Livia and her mother were pleased that I was leaving for Canada and gave me great encouragement.

I had no clothes to leave the country with. What little money I had was needed for food when I reached Canada.   Ann was horrified at my underwear; it was very old or worse, falling apart. I still had some navy blue bloomers left from when I went to school. Ann was so embarrassed that she told me under no circumstances would she allow me to pack any of it in a suitcase that might be opened up by Customs. So we did what I still think of as the most insane smuggling that ever took place.

We opened up Debbie's teddy bear, took out the stuffing and stuffed in all my underwear. Of course we did not tell Ann's four-year-old daughter what we had done to her big teddy bear. We made quite sure she was asleep before we performed the surgery. We imagined we were committing the crime of the century. I thought it was quite ingenious of us. Who would suspect a little girl carrying a fat teddy bear aboard ship of smuggling underwear?

So on April 14, 1960, we said our goodbyes, and I hated it. It seemed so phony, all of us hugging and kissing as though we loved each other. I felt nothing. If there were any feelings, I did not know what they were. I was used to burying them away. I was just itching to get aboard that ship and have a good time.

So at age 18, wearing Ann's clothes, I sailed for Canada on the H.M.S. Ivernia with twelve pounds ten shillings in my purse and my underwear in Debbie's teddy bear.

We were on deck A, cabin number A153. The cabin was small but I loved it. We put the twins on the lower bunk on one side and Debbie on the other lower bunk. I slept above Debbie. For the nine days we were at sea, I felt I was on an enchanted ship. For the first time in my life all the pain left me and I just laughed and had fun. I never for one moment missed anyone and had no fear of what was waiting for me at the end of the journey.

The day after we left Southampton, we docked in France to pick up passengers. The next day we found ourselves on the shores of Ireland picking up more passengers. Everywhere I looked seemed to be emerald green.

On Monday night, again wearing Ann's clothes, we went to the pictures, leaving the ship's nanny to take care of the children. We saw *Summer Place* with Richard Egan and a host of other stars. I thought the film was wonderful. But then,

Hollywood people were the only ones who knew what love was all about.

Tuesday, April 19 was the twins' first birthday. Our steward had a huge cake made for them. Their faces beamed as we lit the candles. As I watched them blow out the candles with the help of their mother, I realized they were going home to their own country, but I had no idea what I was going to. What would become of me? And what would this strange country expect of me? For a moment I felt a dreadful panic, and then Ann interrupted my thoughts.

"Ellen, are you all right? You have gone quite pale."

I said I'd eaten too much and brushed her concern off by singing Happy Birthday to the twins. That was the only moment I allowed my fear to surface. I didn't know why it happened. It just surged into my mind, almost like a warning.

Apart from that awful moment, Ann and I had a wonderful time and we had many a laugh about Debbie's teddy, which she insisted on carrying around everywhere.

Although we were delayed at sea for one day because of fog, on April 20th I saw Newfoundland. The following day I got off in Quebec to show my emigration papers and then got back aboard the ship. On Friday, April 22, I arrived in Montreal, with an unknown future, in an unknown land. I clung to Ann like glue, terrified of getting lost, like a child in the dark.

As I helped Ann look for her trunk among hundreds of others, I noticed the expressions on people's faces. Some seemed happy, as though they could hardly wait to start a new life in this country. But there were others like me, obviously wondering if they had made the right decision. Some women were even weeping. Mothers held onto their children's hands as though to reassure themselves they had made the right choice. Although Don was still away up north for another six months, Ann was frantically searching the crowds of people waiting for friends and relatives. She was hoping her friends would be there to meet us.

After finally finding our luggage, we walked toward the gate, Ann still looking for a familiar face. As I held Michael in my arms, I looked back at the boat and felt a lump in my throat; it had all been so wonderful, so short lived and so very, very safe.

"Ellen, Ellen, I can see them. There they are. See! They're over there."

Of course I couldn't see them. I had never met them. Ann hugged two people who had as thick an accent as we did, although at that time I didn't know I had an accent. I thought it was the Canadians who had one. After all hadn't England been there forever, so how could we have an accent? It turned out this couple was from my own hometown, Brighton.

Miraculously, we all managed to get in the car: four adults, three children, a trunk on the top of the car, luggage piled into the boot and the floor of the car. We were to stay at Raymond and Sue's home, whom Ann had never met. Raymond was up north with Don, and they had become good friends. Sue had offered to put us up for a couple of days until we found an apartment of our own. When I first met Sue, I thought she was very attractive. She was about thirty-six, had short blonde hair, hazel eyes and a stocky build, which somehow suited her bubbly personality.

She turned out to be a guardian angel. Anyone who has a three-bedroom apartment with five children of their own and who takes on two more adults and three more children is either cracked or an angel. She looked after us for four days. We laughed the whole time we all lived together. We had to. We kept falling over one another, or queuing up to go to the toilet. It got so bad that when it was free we would rush to go, just to save having to queue later.

Although Sue was British herself, all her children, except her eldest son, were born in Canada. They were fascinated with my way of speaking and were forever asking me questions just to hear me talk. One of my first culture shocks was witnessing the freedom with which Ann's children spoke to her. At first I thought it was incredibly disrespectful. It took me a while to realize it was part of the Canadian way and that I had been repressed. The love they showed for their mother helped me realize that.

Life in Canada presented me with many shocks. The size of Montreal was scary. A lot more people than I had ever imagined spoke French. Most of the street signs were in French as well as English. The area where we were staying with Sue was called St. Laurent, and we lived on Tasse Street. Ann had to teach me what some of the signs meant, particularly the road sign Arret.

Four days later, Ann and I moved to an apartment on Decarie Boulevard in St. Laurent, not far from Sue. Ann and I made do without furniture. We had only our trunks, a couple of mattresses, some kitchen utensils, blankets and a television. Although we were only there for seven weeks, I had some unforgettable experiences.

Only a couple of weeks after we moved in, the twins got sick, and we had to call the doctor to the house. When I think back and remember the look on the doctor's face, I still want to laugh. Not until the doctor had left did we realize what he had seen: a trunk in the middle of the front room covered with a lace table cloth and a vase of flowers in the center. In the corner was an 'end table'... a suitcase with a lamp on top. In the far corner, on a suitcase, was a television. Our pillows were up against the wall facing the trunk since there was no couch. In Ann's bedroom was a double mattress on the floor and a crib for the twins. The kitchen was furnished with a chair and an ironing board, which we used for a table. My bedroom, which I shared with Debbie, was on the other side of the kitchen. Ann and I agreed that we had doubtless made a great impression on him. At any rate, he gave us free samples of medication for the twins and never sent a bill!

When Sue came over that evening we told her the whole story. As she listened, sitting on a deck chair she had brought over, she looked around the living room.

By the end of the story, she was laughing so hard her deck chair collapsed. With that, we opened up the wine Sue had brought, along with her now-demolished deck chair.

On May 12th, I saw my idol Elvis Presley on a Frank Sinatra show. Wow! What a great country this was. Elvis on TV! After seven weeks, Don arrived home and we moved to an apartment in Pierrefond.

On May 15, 1960, it was Billy's twenty-first birthday. I missed my brother so much. I imagined him having a big party and wondered what country he was in or if he was at home for the biggest birthday of his life. Brits always celebrated well for someone's twenty-first. Dad always thought it was weird that a sixteen-year-old could go to war, carry a gun and shoot to kill, but he couldn't have a pint in the pub until he was twenty-one.

Don took Ann and me on holiday to the United States. "America! We are going to America!"

I was so excited I could hardly breathe. Me, Ellen Blanche Challand, I was actually going to the country where all the rich people live! I had only ever seen pictures of this country and those mostly at cinemas. A dream, come true. "They'll never believe me when I write home about this," I exulted.

We had to show our passports, and I was terrified they wouldn't let us go across the border, but they did. When Don finally stopped the car, I got out very slowly, put my feet firmly on the ground and yelled, "I'm standing on America, everyone!" People stared at me as though I was cracked, but I didn't care what they thought. They were probably Americans and took this country for granted.

We all went to a restaurant to get something to eat. I was not used to eating out, other than in coffee bars, which didn't have menus. With my friends I would just order whatever was written on the board that day, or the standard: chips with salt and vinegar. When I was passed a menu that day, I couldn't understand what I was reading. I said to the waitress, pointing to Don, "I'll have what he's having."

To my embarrassment, she said, "Do you want that medium or rare?"

I had no idea what she was talking about. I turned to Don for help, but he was talking to Ann. I asked the waitress to repeat what she had said, as though I hadn't heard her. Still not understanding her question, and not wanting to admit it, I said: "It doesn't matter."

In a voice that betrayed her annoyance, she snapped: "I can't make up your mind for you. Which is it to be?"

By this time, Don realized what was going on and explained that the waitress wanted to know if I wanted my steak cooked really well or only slightly.

Feeling like a complete fool and wanting to run out of the restaurant, I said, "Cooked well." The waitress looked at me as though I was lacking a brain. I was sure the entire restaurant was staring at me. I still didn't understand why she would bother to ask such a question. Didn't everyone want steaks cooked properly? Why would someone want it cooked just a little bit? Apparently in the United States, rich people were strange about how their food was cooked.

After our holiday I start looking for a job. At my first interview, I couldn't understand why the boss wanted me to go into her office to talk to her. She asked all about my education, as though that had anything to do with work! Then what really made me angry, and which I thought was a complete waste of time, she asked me to fill in a form. Why in hell couldn't things be normal, as in England, where you go in, sign your name and the job's yours. The woman who interviewed me made things very complicated. She didn't even have the decency to call me back to say when I could start work! Other jobs I applied for put me through the same process. I wondered how those kinds of companies could stay in business if they were that fussy about whom they hired.

Eventually, the government found me a job because I had to repay the money I borrowed to emigrate.   On June 3, I found work and was to start the following week. At least when I went there to talk to them they didn't make me fill out a whole pile of forms. They just told me what I would be doing. The wages weren't as good as the other jobs I had applied for, in fact, half as much.   My first pay packet was $28.08 a fortnight, but at least I was able to pay $30.00 back to the government each month and give my sister money for room and board. I didn't go out anywhere, so I didn't need spending money. All I could afford were my cigarettes.

By June 14, Don, Ann and I had moved to Pierrefond, to a house on Basewood Avenue about five miles from Sue. This was my first real home in Canada. It was bigger than the apartment and out in the country. I could look out the kitchen window and see woods for as far as I could see. It reminded me of a place I once loved, Ashurst Road.

I wasn't happy at work because nearly all the girls spoke French. They were always polite and did try to talk to me, but only one spoke English well enough to have a conversation. It made me feel very lonely and left out. It didn't help that I didn't have a good command of the English language. My vocabulary was extremely limited. I began to isolate myself and stopped trying to make friends because I was afraid of making a fool of myself.

"God! I thought I had left all that behind me!" I muttered to myself. I began to miss England, which I had wrongly blamed for all my pain. That tiny island which roared like a lion would be no more for me. Here there was no bluebells growing wild in the woods. There was no ocean with breaking waves.

Homesick, I began to focus on the faults of Canada with its huge cities, hundreds of cars and fast traffic. People would rush by me, hurrying to get somewhere. No time to say hello. Even *bonjour* would have been nice. What did I know about Canada? Nothing! Absolutely nothing! I had never even studied this country in school. I knew more about America than I did of my new homeland. People kept telling me I had an accent and that made me feel like an alien, a foreigner. I thought a foreigner was someone who was staying in a country where they didn't belong.

I gave up going out and trying to socialize because it frightened me too much. It was much easier to stay home with my sister or spend the weekends with Sue, where I felt safe.

On the fourth of July, 1960, my father died. It is a date that will never be without some pain. I did not know how I felt or even what I was supposed to feel. My greatest sadness at the time of his death came from never really having known him. He was a man I lived with for many years, and I didn't even now if he loved me. My fondest memory of him was the day he found out he had cancer. He held me tight and cried for his mother. I didn't know men could cry, especially my father!

Only much later did I begin to understand what a giant of a man he truly was? Understanding came from the pain and fear I experienced in my own life. He was only forty-eight when he first got sick, but he fought it every step of the way and managed to hold on until he died at age fifty-three.

It wasn't so much that he feared death; he had faced that many times, but I believed he began to look over his life -and especially at the lives of his own children. Those must have been the darkest days of my father's life. I fantasized that Dad's mother came to take him to a place of perfect peace.   I know I sincerely wanted my father to have that peace because he found none in his lifetime. It would be five years later when I'd read the diary my father kept of the last year of his life. On one page it read, 'Ellen came back home today. She is so ill and very thin.' We couldn't go back to England for Dad's funeral because we had no money, but Sylvia wrote and told us all about it. With twenty-eight years in the Royal Navy and many more in the Royal Navy Voluntary Reserve, the Sea Cadets gave him a military funeral. As the hearse was driven through the streets, a postman and a policeman stopped and saluted. When Ann read that part to me, I wondered if it was the same policeman who had given me a second chance to life. At the gravesite, Sylvia went on, a White Ensign was draped over his coffin and his naval cap was placed on top, while a cadet played *The Last Post* on a bugle. Mum broke down in church but other wise held up very well. Of my father's children, only Ann and I couldn't attend.

In September that same year, Billy turned up in Montreal. Ann and I were like two children. We were so excited. It was wonderful to see his face. He had only one day; he had to go aboard ship the following morning. He had picked this run especially to see how we were doing. He preferred the South African runs. However, when it came time for him to leave, and he saw how upset Ann and I became, he promised he would come back and visit again.

The following February, we had a terrible snowstorm and lost all our power and water. We brought up all the camping equipment from the locker and cooked on the camp stove, keeping the children in snowsuits and sleeping bags to keep them warm. I felt badly for Ann as she was eight months pregnant, and we were without power for three days. People came around in trucks with water, hot soup and coffee for everyone. Being British we declined the coffee. Ann and I must have drunk more tea in those three days to keep warm than in our entire lives. I couldn't understand why Canadians would drink coffee in a crisis. Brits knew a nice hot cup of tea fixed everything! Of course there had to be piles of sugar in it, otherwise it didn't work.

Ann and Don had another son. Ann took me shopping to help her pick out a coat for her to wear at the christening. We found a beautiful pale green mohair coat for $30.00. After the christening, Ann received the bill for the coat, charged on her account. The bill was for over $100.00. Ann panicked. She ran and looked under the mattress where she hid all her bills from Don. Sure enough, it read $100.00 and some cents.

"Oh my God, Ellen, what am I going to do?"

"Say you didn't know it cost one hundred dollars. No, don't say that, it sounds dumb."

"What am I going to tell Don?"

"We can blame it on the store. We will tell Don they tricked us into thinking it was only $30.00."

"Ellen don't you understand, Don will kill me if he thought I paid thirty dollars for a coat. I told him I only paid twenty for it, and he wasn't pleased about that."

"Ask for a divorce."

"Funny Ellen, very funny."

"Not really, Ann, because when he finds out how much you paid for the coat, he's going to ask you for a divorce anyway. But by asking him first, you can always look back in your old age and say you beat him to it."

"I need your brains, not your rotten humor."

"Well you're out of luck on two accounts; one, I don't think my humor is rotten and two, I have no brains. After all, look at it from my point of view. I came thousands of miles to start a new life in a country paved with gold! What do I get instead? Snow storms, no electricity, and no water and in the summer we all fry. As if that's not enough, I am helping my sister find a bill for a coat that should have cost $20.00 but actually cost $30.00; but then, it really cost over $100.00. Now you want me to help you cover up the crime you committed which I thought you had already done by hiding the bill under the very mattress Don sleeps on. Just out of sheer curiosity, what are all these other bills under the mattress?"

As I said that and reached for the other bills, Ann dropped the mattress on top of me and stormed out of the room.

We never did tell Don. But we returned the coat to the store and found the price tag that was originally on the coat. It read thirty dollars.

I learned one thing from all that: how easy it was to buy anything you wanted with a piece of plastic. I could hardly wait to write home and tell my friends what a rich country this was, that people didn't have to get paid right away to buy something. Almost everyone had phones, fridges, cars and televisions. Ann even had a bank account. I had never known anyone who had a bank account. I hoped I would never have to go inside a bank. I knew it would scare me to death.

In July 1962, we went on another holiday. This time to the southern States, an experience I would never forget. The black people were the friendliest people I had ever met. So it was difficult for me to understand how anyone could shun them. On a couple of occasions, Ann and I accidentally walked into toilets for black women only. As young and immature as I was, I felt fear and confusion as to why anyone would treat a person disrespectfully because of their color. It wasn't just being uncomfortable with what I saw, but something I felt much deeper within myself. There was a sadness I could not explain. I felt like apologizing to all the black people for so much ignorance. There was a look in their eyes, almost asking, "Do you really believe you're better than me?" If they only knew how I felt about myself. Everybody was better than me.

In the nearly fourteen months since I had arrived in Canada, much had happened - some good, some bad - which I supposed was a part of life. I wouldn't have put it down to a learning experience, as I was far too immature to see that clearly. I rarely went out of the house unless it was to go to work. Most of my time was spent watching television with Ann.   We had four favorite programs. Mine was "Rawhide" because I was in love with the guy named Yates. When he appeared in a spaghetti western, I learned his real name was Clint Eastwood.

Ann and I were good company for each other because Don was away most of the time, either studying at McGill University or in his bedroom. He wanted to get his degree, but I didn't understand what that meant, other than he must be very clever to be going to university. I remembered Don and Ann having an argument over how much schooling we had. At that time Don said we wouldn't pass grade seven. What was so ironic about that remark was I felt complimented. I had seen some of Sue's children's homework, and knew I couldn't pass grade five.

On my twentieth birthday, I sat on my bed going through my old black vanity case I had brought with me from England, reminiscing about the past months in Canada. I noticed the brooch I bought on the Ivernia, the ship that had brought me to my new life. My mind swam with questions. Would I ever see England again and what future, if any, had the Ivernia brought me to?

CHAPTER 8

Dreams and Broken Promises

His name was Andrew Szita. My brother-in-law introduced him to me shortly after we had come back from our holidays. His hair was very dark, but thinning. He had a round face, full lips and incredible blue eyes. On our first date, we went to New York State, spent the day on the beach and in the evening went to a drive-in movie. I was crazy about drive-ins. To me they were the most wonderful inventions in the world. Andrew and I had met in August; by November we planned to marry and were engaged on Christmas Day in 1961.

It wasn't that I was madly in love with Andy, but he was a gentle soul, reliable and undemanding. He wasn't violent and that made him a refuge, a sanctuary. He had completed grade twelve at school and even had two years of college! Me! Yes, me, marrying a bloke that went to college. What more could any woman want of a man! Wasn't he a dream come true? I wasn't passing this one up. I did that once before and regretted it. For once in my life, I'll make my mother happy. She would brag to everyone and have the neighbors believing he was a professor by the time she was finished.

Andrew's parents came from Hungary. While he was a small child, his mother died in a car accident in Montreal. After his mother was killed, Andy went to live with some relatives who brought him up.

Andrew and I were married in Saint Andrew's Church in Montreal on July 14, 1962. The priest told me I was never to use birth control. There was no way I wanted to end up like my mother with eight children. On March 31, 1963, at three minutes past midnight, my daughter Kim was born.

I had very much wanted to breastfeed Kim, but it was not to be. I couldn't manage it with any of my children. And even though it was not my fault, I felt secretly a failure: something else to add to the list. I'll never forget the panic I felt bringing Kim home from the hospital. She was all of seven pounds nine ounces, a living, breathing human being. Kim was so small and dependent on me. Me! I could hardly take care of myself!

She slept right by my bedside in a basket because I was sure she would stop breathing. I practically lived at Ann's house and sometimes even stayed overnight. Andy didn't mind too much because he was on night shift and had to sleep during the day. Ann was wonderful in helping me with Kim. The two of us became very close. Only much later in life did I realize that, although I was very close to my brothers and sisters, none of us shared our emotional pain. I have often wondered if we even knew what our pain was.

One afternoon, Kim, who was just three weeks old, was sleeping in her crib in the bedroom, and I was ironing in the living room. At that time, Andy and I were living in the basement suite at my mother-in-law's house, and Andy had built some heavy-duty shelves and put them up on the wall in the bedroom. These shelves held everything imaginable, from four-gallon jugs of wine we had made to Andy's tools.

This particular afternoon, I had a sudden irrational and intense anxiety. I knew it concerned Kim. Putting the iron down, I ran in to where Kim lay in her crib. Though she was fast asleep and quite safe, the fear would not leave. Cautiously, I pulled the crib to the middle of the room. I went back into the living room to continue ironing, telling myself off for being stupid.

Suddenly, I heard the most incredible crashing sound from the bedroom. Rushing into the room, I almost gagged at what I saw. All three shelves had ripped right out of the wall and everything had smashed everywhere, right where Kim's crib had been. Visualizing what would have happened to Kim if I had not moved the crib upset me for days. There was no explanation as to why my inner voice gave me that warning.

That was not the only time I experienced such a phenomenon. A couple of months later I was cleaning house, and I was certain I heard my brother

Billy call out to me as though he were in the next room. I knew immediately something was wrong and that he was in pain, but to tell someone that would have sounded insane so I kept telling myself, No! No! It's just me missing him.

A couple of days later, Ann phoned me. She had received a letter from England. Billy was in hospital because a car had run him down, and both his legs were broken. When I told Ann of my premonition, she wasn't surprised. Over the next six years, Ann and I both would hear our inner voices a few times, even in our dreams.

One November afternoon, as Kim was asleep and I sorted laundry in the living room, I watched a thriller movie on television. When a bulletin came on to say there had been some sort of accident with President Kennedy, I didn't pay much attention, except to call up the stairs to my mother-in-law to complain about how annoyed I was that they cut into my film. I tried changing channels to find another program, but all the stations had the same news. Then I started to feel scared. Why did all the channels have it on if it was nothing to worry about? I called my mother-in-law because I suddenly didn't want to be on my own. Once Walter Cronkite made the announcement, choking back the tears as he did so, I knew it was true. President Kennedy was dead. I couldn't imagine how something like that could possibly happen in America.

As I watched the funeral, I wondered if this kind of tragedy could cause some sort of war, and I was afraid. I kept looking into the crib at my baby daughter, wondering what the future would hold for her. It was then that I finally broke down and cried.

Sylvia wanted me to go back to England with her for a visit. I was so unhappy with my life that Andy wanted me to go for a while. I questioned Andy on what would happen if going home did not cure my unhappiness. What if I wanted to stay in England and not come back to Canada? But he said not to worry about that unless it happened.

That made me realize something about me: I always worried about what might happen and put a lot of energy into that worry. I believe the unhappiness had a lot to do with low self esteem and feeling very inadequate. Canada was a different country, a different culture, with different expectations from England. I felt out of place here, and I couldn't do anything right. My lack of education began to creep into my thoughts regularly, and I always had excuses about why I didn't need one. I worked hard at staying in denial, perhaps my life's worst lie. I wouldn't see the pain my ignorance was causing me. It played heavily on my emotions, getting in the way of any hope for a happy future.

The day after Sylvia and I arrived in England, Kim turned two years old. It was my first plane trip. I was exhausted from the flight and had no idea it would take so long.

We came home to find Anthony living in a boy's school called Saint Edward's in Sheffield and Joan was living in, Saint John's School, in Birmingham.

According to Anthony, only fourteen, he was

living there because Mother found it impossible to work and look after him at the same time. Mum would often be gone overnight because of the type of work she did, she was a silver service waitress. Mum would travel all over the country, even to London, to wait on people at various events, such as banquets or cricket matches, and functions involving royalty, like Ascot. If she came home in the evening, it was often nine or ten at night. What with Anthony having his mother put him in a strange place and then losing a father who doted on him, I could see how Anthony felt abandoned. He must have felt abandoned by all of us with, Ann, Sylvia and I all in Canada, Billy and Bobby in the merchant navy and Joan in another city, too far away for him to even visit. I was not surprised that he ended up in trouble.

Joan, now sixteen, had also been put away, and her story was just as heartbreaking. She said she had been waiting for a cheque in the mail from a company she had previously worked for. It never turned up. When she went down to the company to find out what the delay was, they told her not only had the cheque gone out weeks ago, but it had also been signed for. It wasn't hard to recognize the scribbled signature as they showed her the form.

Angry and disbelieving, she went directly home to confront Mother. Finding the house empty and unable to get rid of her pain, she took all the money out of the gas meter. Even though Joan was wrong in what she did, no judge in the world would have ever put her away if they had known the whole truth. But she felt the need to protect that person just like the rest of us. She never knew why. It wasn't the first time theft had taken place in the house, and we were all partly to blame by remaining silent. It wasn't even fear anymore that held us back; it was fixed in our minds over the years that was the way it had to be.

It was wrong! Horribly wrong! Yet many children would pay the tragic price of their parents' sins, and many would spend their lives wondering if anyone cared, as they lived with the emotional scars of being innocent and found guilty. In essence, they spent the rest of their lives in a prison, whether it was behind bars or in the heart of the soul, paying the price for someone else's emotional scars. It was a vicious circle of hate and silence passed on from one generation to another. "Dear God," I wondered, "where will it all end, and what chance is there for the ugliness to ever stop?"

I managed to get Anthony home for a few days, but they wouldn't let Joan out to have a visit. Anthony loved Kim. He carried her everywhere, putting her on rides, taking her to the beach, buying her sweets, and sitting on the floor and playing with her for hours. I came to love Anthony dearly in that short period of time, and it pained me to see the way people treated him. He was not full fare on the bus because he was only fourteen, but Anthony was six feet tall and everyone questioned him about his age. I saw by the look in their eyes or heard the cutting comments they would make. No one believed him. He once told me he often paid full fare so he was not harassed. I talked to him about it, but he laughed and said it was not so bad because when he and the blokes at the hostel went for a walk, he would sneak into the shops for the blokes and buy them cigarettes. You could only buy cigarettes if you were sixteen, so he felt he got his own back for all the nasty comments. So much was expected of Anthony just because he was so tall. By the time he reached twenty-one, Anthony stood six foot four.

While in England, I visited my cousin Mary, and we spent many pleasant hours together. While rocking Kim back and fourth and chatting over a cup of tea, she said,

"Tell me something Ellen, do you ever remember your parents holding you on their laps as you're doing with Kim right now?"

Her question stunned me. My love for Kim was without thought, and I couldn't imagine not holding her in my arms, playing with her on the floor or trying to make her laugh. Yet here was a question which unlocked the door to many more that I didn't want to think about.

Although my feelings on how much I loved Kim were never in question, my being a good mother was. When Kim became too much for me, I didn't hesitate putting her in the playpen, where she probably spent far too many hours. I felt guilty, but rather than deal with the question as to why, I let it continue. I preferred to watch television rather than take her for a walk, and she was often left in her wet diaper too long.

Often, when it came to feeding her, and if no one was around to watch me, I would put her food in a bottle, make a bigger hole in the nipple and let her feed herself, so I didn't have to spoon feed her. What was love to me? If Kim was love, it frightened me because I knew she was someone I would give my life for, and it had nothing to do with being brave. It was by nature that I had such feelings for her. Hadn't I carried her in my womb for nine months? Yet Mary's question plagued me.

No! My parents never sat me on their lap or told me that they loved me. For the first time, I realized a child can be living with their parents and still be abandoned.

Later that same day, Mary and I went to see where my father was buried. I couldn't define my feelings when seeing his grave. I half expected him to come out and hit me. I realized my fear of him was still there. That was dreadfully upsetting. I was afraid of a dead man! Was it because the conflict between Mother and me was still going on? Only the previous day while in her kitchen, an argument broke out, and she threatened to hit me. Anthony startled me by threatening Mother if she dared to even come close. I was perplexed by Anthony's anger and awed that he would stick up for me. Few people had ever stood up for me, and in that passing moment my love for Anthony was overpowering. Feeling worthwhile was wonderful, but the circumstances it took to make me feel that way were ludicrous.

When I finally left England to return to Canada, it was with a very heavy heart. Sylvia didn't come back with me. She had decided to take a job as a nanny in another part of England. All the pain I had thought was in the past was very much alive deep within me, like cancerous roots that I didn't have the strength to pull up and throw away. Perhaps I'd always known the pain was still there, but denial and repression was my shield.

Andy was at the airport to meet Kim and me, and as he waved to us, the thought crossed my mind: "Who is this man I'm married to?" He knew I had conflicts, but he never questioned them. Sometimes I hoped he would. Something; Anything! For instance, why did I get so upset about him going to the fridge after supper? I'd get so angry watching him help himself to food. It was as though we were on rations. As a child, I had been slapped if I ever went to the pantry to help myself, but then most times it was locked. Slapping Andy would never have crossed my mind. My anger when he took food from the fridge whenever he felt like it was unjustified.

I also wondered why he'd never question me about my illiteracy. It was too painful for me to bring it up, and perhaps in my heart the wish was that he hadn't really noticed.   Andy never questioned me about anything, making me realize he was unable to cope with dysfunctional or emotional situations. This left me feeling isolated. He knew sex was a real problem for me, but he said nothing. It was two years into our marriage before I could ever enjoy sex, and that was only through a friend who gave me a book to read. A book I read with great difficulty because my reading was so poor. No matter which way I turned, I felt a failure, especially about not making Andy happy.

Soon after returning from England, I began to have nightmares. They were always the same. I was with my cousin Mary standing in an oval room full of coffins. They were placed in a row and had the same oval shape as the room. The coffins were made of a beautiful wood with purple and white satin on the inside. My father lay in one of them. The one that was empty I knew was mine. Through the windows shone a ray of sunshine, but it only shone on half the room. The other half was in darkness, and that was where my coffin lay. Was it a message I was wasting space on this earth? I longed to tell

Andy, but I didn't think he'd understand.   Why would he? I didn't!

The other dream was always set in England. I would be standing in a sunlit field full of the most beautiful flowers of all different colors. I'd be wearing ragged clothes and trying hopelessly to find food for Kim because she was starving. Even in the dream, I tried to understand why my baby was starving to death while everything around me was so beautiful.

In my dreams, as in life, I felt like a failure. It seemed there was no escape. I had promised to love, honor and obey. But because of my inadequacy and low self-worth, my marriage vows were broken even before they were made.

CHAPTER 9

Children of a Stormy Harvest

This period of my life I would remember as being one of my worst, and the precious seed inside of me would pay the price. I was pregnant again.

We had moved from my mother-in-law's suite to an apartment on Ridgewood Avenue, off Cote des Neiges in Montreal. Andy and I took part time jobs as janitors of the building in order to have free rent. It seemed the only way we could survive because, although Andy was working for Bell Canada, he was new at his job, and his cheque was not enough for us to live on.

Our apartment was a basement suite. Our windows were almost level with the street. During this pregnancy, I was so ill that I spent a lot of time lying down in our bedroom. At rush hour the traffic would be at a standstill, the exhaust fumes seeping into our basement. Years later I realized why I had been so ill. No one had thought of the amount of carbon monoxide coming through my bedroom window. I felt ill. And when lying down, I felt worse and just stayed there. I had been feeling totally defeated ever since I'd seen my father's grave. How could I still be afraid of my father? He was dead.

But even my love for Kim couldn't hold me together anymore. I was falling apart. Being married should have solved all my problems, but I simply didn't have the ability to think clearly.

I stopped going over to Ann's house, using the excuse it was too far. Everything I ate tasted vile, and I could no longer smoke a cigarette. I couldn't even drink tea. My thoughts raced everywhere, as though trying desperately to find a reason to continue. I had no idea why I was feeling so desperate. I remembered my parents being very unhappy people and my mother forever threatening suicide.

That's when it first occurred to me: it must be genetic. The thought of feeling like this forever was too much, and I began to sink farther and farther into myself. Andy became so concerned he called my doctor, but he put it down to my hard pregnancy.

Meanwhile, I started planning to kill myself.

Andy was working night shift. I could take my life after he went to work. Kim was in bed, but I don't remember putting her there. I had a bath, and for some odd reason, washed my hair. After putting my nightie on, I climbed into bed. All the pills I could find in the house were on the night table, and I had purchased a large bottle of Aspirin as well.

Since this was the last thing I would ever do, I wanted to make sure I did something right before leaving. I started taking the Aspirins first, one-by-one. For some reason, my hand kept resting on my tummy. I was worried about whether the baby would feel any pain.

While I was taking my fifth or sixth aspirin, an incredible fatigue overtook me. So overwhelming was the tiredness, that I laid my head back on my pillow and began to feel a peaceful sadness. Then something quite odd happened. A comforting warmth came over me, and my mind reflected back to when I was a child. I'd only experienced that type of warmth before in a dream, but this was no dream. I was awake. I could smell the scent of roses. It was so strong, it was almost overpowering. My eyes began to close and just when I might have felt frightened, I felt someone take my hand. It was so warm and gentle, like velvet. My eyes did not open; I didn't try to open them or even want to. Opening my eyes might make the peace I was feeling leave me, and I wanted it to last forever. I fell into a deep sleep, and was awakened by the sound of Andy calling me.

"Ellen, are you all right? Do you know what time it is? It's almost eight o'clock. What in heaven's name are all those pills doing there?"

My mind was in a fog. I wasn't even sure what had happened the night before. Explaining it to Andy was definitely out; he'd be sure I had cracked up. Had I? It was Andy's next question that shook me fully awake.

"Where did the roses come from?"

"What roses, I don't see any roses."

"Neither do I, but the whole room smells of them."

I remembered the pills by my bed. "Maybe it's coming from outside. Have a look out the window Andy." I needed to put all the pills away before he remembered to ask me about them.

At that moment Kim came out of her bedroom. It was unusual for her to sleep that long, but I was happy she had. I put the pills back on the table and went to hold Kim tight. I was so glad to still be here, even if it were just for Kim.

She put her hand on my tummy, and in her childish way, asked me if I was sick. It was then I realized I hadn't thrown up that morning. As Andy turned from the window, his eyes rested on the pills again.

Very stupidly I said, "My head was aching last night."

"Must have been a hell of a headache," was all he said.

There was no magic, no miracle and nothing changed, but the thought of suicide had disappeared. I was left with guilt: the guilt of not having thought enough about Kim and the baby I was carrying.

After I had put the pills back in the bathroom cupboard, I turned and walked into the kitchen to find Kim standing on a chair. She had taken out the jar of jam and was spooning it straight into her mouth; she was far too busy to notice me. I leaned up against the kitchen door and watched her. Kim's greatest feature was her large, light brown eyes. With jam all over her chin and down her nightie, I noticed what an angelic face she had, round and chubby, framed with short, light brown hair.

I'll never know what happened that night, and I trusted no one enough to talk about it, not even Ann. Whatever it was, I learned how deeply I loved Kim. It also left me aware of an empty and lonely place inside of me, a place my parents had failed to fill. Having grown to adulthood with this empty place, I was like a child in an adult's body. Always, I was searching for something lost, never really knowing what. I wondered how many other lives like mine were out there in the world. Lost, stumbling, in a dark and lonely place, groping through life, longing to be found. It is an agony that cannot cry out. The broken heart must remain silent.

On March 15, 1966 my son Anthony was born. His was a very difficult birth, almost as though it went hand-in-hand with how ill I had been during the entire pregnancy. The doctor picked Anthony up and put him in my arms. To my horror, I realized I didn't want to hold him. I was rejecting him. The doctor could see what was happening and tried to assure me that I wouldn't have another labor like that. He didn't understand the rejection went much deeper.

I didn't really understand it myself. Didn't I want a son? Yes, but not another
baby I had to be responsible for. What if he grew up feeling all the pain I was feeling? I didn't want to be

responsible for that kind of pain. I had seen my father's grave, but still I was afraid of him. I had seen my brother Anthony and my sister Joan put away in a strange place, lost and alone.

The war in Viet Nam was raging and young men were dying by the thousands. If they went to war, their own people damned them; if they didn't, the government damned them. What kind of pain must their loved ones be going through? How many families would be forever trying to heal the wounds? And how many soldiers, once again, would die or be forever scarred emotionally and physically? Why? Why was the world so cruel?

Andy was thrilled he had a son, and I hoped he would be Anthony's saving grace.

By the time I was expecting my third child; I had moved twice and was now living in a basement suite in a large complex north of Montreal. It should have been called *Peyton Place*. I could write a book on the three and a half years I lived there. Billy and his new wife Jackie immigrated to Montreal. She was seventeen and Bill was twenty-eight. Sylvia was living in Washington D.C. Ann had bought a house and seemed content to play the role of wife and mother.

Our second son, Robert, arrived on February 1st, 1968. By the end of that year, Martin Luther King Jr. and Robert Kennedy were both dead. Gone. Their deaths seemed to mark the end of a great era. It seemed to me that Satan was alive and that the whole world had gone insane. The use of illicit drugs was on the rise; no one worked at their marriages any more and divorce was common. It appeared sex was in and love didn't matter anymore. There seemed no awareness of morality.

There were beatniks and hippies high on flower power. And there were others who were trying to hold on to what was once sane. The music was wild, although some of it was wonderful, with meaningful words. Every weekend there seemed to be a party somewhere. I felt like we were all running from the discontent that seemed pervasive.

In my own city of Montreal, there was great unrest among the French Canadians. I had great difficulty understanding any of it, but like most, I just thought it was all a fad that would eventually fade away.

As I cut the cake for Robert's first birthday, I hoped he would be my last baby. If I hadn't been so stupid and let someone else tell me how to run my life, I wouldn't have gotten pregnant again. When I asked the doctor for birth control pills, he said: "You're a Catholic, shouldn't you talk to your priest first?" And like the idiot I was, that was the end of that.

I couldn't believe it when I got pregnant again. This was too much for me. No, I wasn't going through this agony again. I didn't want another child; I couldn't look after the three I had. Although the house was very clean, I spent a lot of time sleeping and hated getting up in the morning. It was not unusual for Kim to go out to play without having breakfast first. Kim would play outside, and I never worried about checking on her. Anthony was a mother's dream; he always occupied himself and never made demands on me. I suppose he learned early to take care of himself, since I rarely picked him up and held him. Even when he was a newborn, I would prop him up in his crib with his bottle, rather than hold him in my arms.

My friend Mary was right. I couldn't have another baby. It was just too much. I talked it over with Andy, and he agreed if I wanted an abortion, it was up to me. After I phoned the doctor, I called my friend back and told her the doctor would do it the following Friday. I felt frantic that I had to wait a week, but the doctor was going on holidays.

"Bloody hell!" I sputtered to myself. A whole damned week to go, and the thoughts of Mary, Mother of Jesus, kept creeping into my mind. I do wish she would mind her own bloody business! Anyhow, where was she when I needed her most? Did she protect me when I was a little girl? No! All she ever did was come to me in my dreams. Well I was having an abortion, no matter what she thought about it!"

But she wouldn't leave me alone. I'd see her in my dreams holding baby Jesus. One night I woke up crying from a dream in which I stood alone in the middle of a room full of people. They were having a party, but it was as though I didn't exist. The loneliness was overwhelming, and as I looked around the room, I saw a picture of 'Our lady' on the wall; she smiled at me and said, "I am the mother of all children." I'd had the same dream when I lived in the orphanage. That night I told her, "Okay, if you don't want me to have an abortion, you change my mind for me." She did. The guilt left me.

Carolann was born November 19, 1969. I was determined to have no more children, so I had some strange thing inserted inside me. Some called it a coil and others called it an umbrella. I never questioned the doctor. After all, he had the degree. Who was I to question a man with so much education?

The crisis in Quebec was now totally out of hand. Bombs were being planted in unexpected places, even in mailboxes. Andy and I made tentative plans to move to British Columbia. Andy wasn't as keen as I, but when I saw parent's fistfighting outside of Kim's school, I made up my mind; we had to leave. Making such a decision was rather surprising to me. I never thought of myself as having the courage or stamina to make such a move.

We headed for British Columbia in July of 1970. Mustering all my physical and emotional strength, I was taking my beautiful seeds; my children who were growing so fast now, to a new place of hope, away from the storm that was brewing. I had come to Quebec to start a new life, but it had not happened for me. Now it never would. All I had was the hope I could protect my babies long enough to see them reap the life I would never have.

CHAPTER 10

Hope Beyond The Mountains

We set out for B.C. in our old blue 1963 Ford station wagon, rusted from the salt of many winters. We laughed about all the things we had packed, even leftover food, but I knew in my heart we were both afraid of not finding a job in B.C. Andy was hoping for something with British Columbia's telephone company, but we didn't even know if they were hiring.

What would British Columbia be like? I wondered if the people would be friendly. I missed the British and their ways. In England you could stand at a bus stop and know a person's whole life story in the ten minutes it took for the bus to arrive.

The children were excited about moving, and as I listened to them, memories of my emigration came flooding back. The distance we were moving now was the same as when I had left England. It was like emigrating all over again.

As we traveled across the country, the heat in the car was almost unbearable, and we had to keep stopping. One evening, Andy decided to keep on driving because it was much cooler at night. I turned toward the back of the car and looked at the faces of my children as they slept. The two boys were laid out in the very back with their pillows and blankets. No matter what the heat, not unlike me, four-year-old Anthony had to have a blanket to sleep with. He and his two-year-old brother Robert were holding onto their teddy bears. Seven-year-old Kim was sleeping across the seat behind Andy and me. Carolann, seven months old, was asleep between us in the front seat. All our baggage was on top of the car on the roof rack.

I felt apprehensive as we drove through the dark to an unknown future. I had pushed Andy into this move. What if he didn't get a job? Where would we go and how would we eat? Thank God we at least had friends we could stay with when we arrived. My hand was hurting from clutching my rosary so tightly. Ann had bought me a beautiful rosary as a farewell gift. I have only ever had two in my life, and she had given me both.

British Columbia was indeed beautiful. The mountains soared, encircling us. We were in awe. Seeing God's creation all around us, I felt an emotion I hadn't experienced before. Perhaps the mountains knew something I did not. It was as though they were stretching their arms out, beckoning to me. Joy swept over me although I still felt apprehensive. Whatever my feelings at that moment, I knew one thing: I was home. At long last, I was home! It was as though I had found my roots.

The first six weeks were really rough. We put every penny we had into rent. Andy did not get hired right away, and we were both very frightened. But one day after several weeks had gone by, B.C. Tel called asking Andy to start work. Slowly our lives started to pick up. Andy went on night shift, and that was hard on him since Kim was the only one in school, and it was difficult to keep the other three quiet. I often felt a sense of guilt that four children were too much for Andy to cope with. But somehow he seemed to manage.

By early October, Trudeau had declared martial law in Quebec. So it was no surprise to learn Billy had gone back to England or to see Bobby and Jean arrive on our doorstep a few months later. Bobby and Jean managed to find a place to live in the same complex as us, but it was a long time before Bobby found a stable job. I had missed Bobby a lot. We had grown close since his arrival in Canada. He could always make everybody laugh. Sometimes we would talk until three or four in the morning, reminiscing about our teenage years. His version seemed funny and wilder in comparison to mine. But I noticed Billy was always featured somewhere when things were at their funniest.

My favorite story of Bobby's was when he was dating Jean and trying to make a good impression since Jean was considered quite the lady.

Before he dated her, he used to watch her walk up the road. They lived on the same street, and Bobby would make comments as she passed by. "Look at old toffee nose! Isn't your nose cold, stuck up in the air that far, darling?"

On his first date with Jean, he took her out for tea. His wild friends and Billy went along. Everything was going well until one of the friend's orders was given to a bloke at the next table. John asked for his food back, but the man decided he liked what he saw and told John where to go. That was a mistake, and the gentleman found himself wearing the food. Then all hell broke loose.

Bobby stuffed Jean under the table, and between the crashing of the chairs and fists flying everywhere, the boys managed to find the cake tray. To this day, the blokes all swore the lemon meringue pies whirled the best and that Bobby swung better than anyone. It seemed he not only spun the pies well but also hit his target right on. Hearing the police arriving, Billy ran out to direct them to the wrong restaurant, giving the boys time to escape out the back door. Bobby ran back to grab Jean who was still hiding under the table. Once they were all outside, Billy phoned for a taxi; but as he shifted to ask the boys how many taxis were needed, the cord snapped off the phone box. Bobby grabbed the phone with the cord still dangling, took Jean with the other hand and ran off down the road. Jean fell for the blonde-headed, blue-eyed bloke just the same.

When I first met Caroline she was taking the washing over to the Laundromat. She had just moved in next door to Bobby and Jean. As I looked at her, thinking what an attractive women she was, I had no idea what an impact she would have on my life. It was as though until I had met her, my life had been lost in 'what I should do' and not 'what I could do'. Over the months she inspired me greatly, and I came to trust and love her as no other friend.

In our first conversation Caroline said, "Let's have a party". And it seemed to me to last forever. One of my favorite parties at Caroline's was the time

I decided to go for a walk. But Caroline's husband John, who was every bit as adorable as she was, didn't want me to go alone. So it ended up Andy, John and I went for a walk with the music of Neil Diamond's "Red, Red Wine" playing in the background. I found a child's tricycle at the top of someone's driveway. I just had to ride it. But I had not counted on John and Andy helping me in their very highly inebriated state. I had pushed the tricycle to the top of Caroline's steep driveway, when the guys gave me one big push down the drive. I lost control of the only vehicle I had ever driven in my life. I was headed straight for the garage door. As I picked up speed to what seemed about eighty miles an hour, I tried desperately to slam on the brakes, but having never driven a three-wheeler before, and I didn't know there weren't any. My head reached the garage door first, and my feet flew up over my head. I thought I had gone blind until I realized my dress had fallen down and wrapped itself around my face.

The screams of laughter from Andy and John were short-lived when Caroline came running out of the house to see what the noise was all about. When she saw the state I was in, she blasted the two of them in her usual feisty way, giving them what-for.

"John, you are to stop laughing this instant! Do you hear me?"

"Yes, Caroline, my darling, anything you say."

"You're still laughing, John."

"It's not my fault, look at Andy! He's just about peeing in his pants. And it's his wife."

"Andy, stop laughing and help me get your wife's legs down from the garage door. John, I want that bike taken back immediately!"

"Yes, my darling, whatever you say. I'll return whatever is left of the bike; at least it's more than what's left of Ellen."

With that, Andy and John sat down on the ground and laughed so loud one of the neighbors complained. Caroline had to drag them both inside to shut them up.

Andy and I bought a house in Ladner, a new development in the suburbs of Vancouver, not far from where John and Caroline bought theirs. In the back of our house at the end of the garden, there was a field of corn as far as I could see. Sometimes I stood transfixed watching it blowing back and forth in the wind. It looked like an ocean of pure gold. These were moments when I was sure the painful past was behind me. This was my happy ending.

And then I found out I was pregnant again.

CHAPTER 11

Laughter In The Face Of The Enemy

This was a nightmare. Andy had had a vasectomy months ago. How could I possibly be pregnant? I would wake up any minute and laugh about it, wouldn't I? I should have made him go back to have the testing done to be sure it had taken. Now it was too late.

The doctor said, "I'll get you into the hospital as soon as I can and give you a hysterectomy." He went on, "Even if you decide to go through with this, you will probably miscarry and that could cause more problems because your womb is in such bad shape. You also have to take into consideration that you have been on several different kinds of medication for the past few months and that might have affected the fetus."   "Amazing," I thought to myself, how it's always a fetus when the subject is abortion. Why can't people be honest and say, 'a baby'! That's what it is, a new life being formed. Why didn't I have a hysterectomy when the doctor first wanted me to? I've made another mistake! I'm stupid. I should have taken more responsibility for my own body. I hate all this confusion. I don't know what's right or wrong anymore. Some condemn abortion, and some condone it. But how can anyone condone abortion if there are all kinds of birth control pills out there? What about people like me whose faith doesn't allow abortion?   What if a woman was raped?   Would that make abortion right? I don't even have the right to an opinion. I'm so stupid and uneducated. I'm too inhibited to give my opinion. I wouldn't want People, coming down on me more than life already has.

I stood in the kitchen the following morning in my long gold housecoat, feeling nauseated. Andy was doing the dishes.

"Andy, I have thought seriously about this surgery, and I want to know how you would feel if I refused to have it done until after the baby's born."

"You must be out of your mind. You can't handle the four kids you have! What about all the pills you've been taking? Even if you did make it, and the baby was born, what state would it be in?"

"But we don't know that for sure, Andy. To be perfectly truthful, I want to take my chances and have this child. I just don't see abortion being morally right for me."

"For you! What about us? There are five other people living in this house besides you. If you want to talk about honesty, let me be honest. I don't want a fifth child."

Never had I heard Andy talk like that to me before, and the truth was I felt he was right. I was having enough troubles handling the four I had. God knows we couldn't afford another, what with the new house and car. The bills were piling up and just about choking us. So the deed was done.

My shame was that once again I'd let others tell me what I should do with my body and how I should think and feel. That's the way it had always been, somebody telling me what to do. But it was easy for them. They didn't have to live with the memories. I would look at Carolann and remember how close I had come to losing her and how much she meant to me now.

When Caroline asked me if I wanted to work with her at a mushroom farm, I was overjoyed. She assured me that there was nothing to it and I didn't even have to fill out an application or have an interview. It sounded like the perfect job and a solution to some of our financial problems. At least I'd be doing my part, whatever that was.

I loved working there, especially with Caroline. Often on a short working day, she would drive me back to my house and stay for a while. We would get out the wine, and she would tell me all the wonderful things she was going to teach me to do. Most important was to teach me to drive. She said that would give me some independence. While she talked to me, she would be on my kitchen floor doing her push-ups. She encouraged me to believe I could do all things, if I tried: learning to drive, making decisions for myself. She'd tell me the positive things that I could do, like cooking for six people, caring for my children, how she admired my house always being clean, how I never failed to pick up Carolann from school on time, how well dressed the children always were, allowing the children to have a dog, cats, mice and fish in the home. She taught me to laugh. She believed in me when I did not. But, oh, I wanted to!

What she didn't know, and I didn't tell her, was one of my great failures to my children was not being able to help them with their homework.

One day after work, as we sat in my house drinking a glass of wine, Caroline came up with the brilliant idea to perm my hair. Still in her farm clothes, she took off to the store to buy what we needed. Half way through doing my hair, we ran out of perm solution. Out she went again to buy some more. By the time we were finished with my hair, we were on our second bottle of wine. When Caroline saw the finished product, there was a long silent pause. Then she asked me if I was planning to go to Africa because I would blend in quite nicely! Surprise! I loved my Afro and kept it for a long time.

Mondays were my son Robert's favorite day because I'd bake bread and doughnuts. He'd hurry home from school, running into the house, so anxious to help. He was the most beautiful child a mother could have. I actually worried about him being outside on his own because people stopped him in the street to talk to him. He was chubby, with pale skin that seemed to enhance his dark eyes and black hair. He had a large dimple in his chin, a smile that would steal anyone's heart and the most contagious laugh.

One Monday, as he ran into the house throwing his jacket to the floor, he put his chubby little hands upon the counter and just managed to rest his chin there. This was the greatest day of Robert's childhood. He had never seen such large doughnuts.

Of course Caroline and I had been into the wine, a very dry wine so we wouldn't gain weight. As usual, I had more to drink than she. Caroline always knew when to stop. So we were feeling very merry when she offered to help me make the bread and doughnuts. She taught me a lot about cooking, along with Andy who was a great cook too.

"I think I put too much yeast in the doughnuts, Ellen. What do you think?"

"You put yeast in too! I thought you told me to do that."

Caroline thought hard, "Well, you could always use the doughnuts as loaves of bread."

Poor Robert, he had no idea why we were laughing so heartily.

"No Mum, don't listen to Aunty Caroline; I like them big like that."

I told him not to worry, and that I would put one in his school lunch everyday.

When Caroline left, I went through Robert's school bag. He had some homework, but I was too busy to help him with that. Then in came Kim and Anthony with their homework too.

"Mum, you have to help me with my homework, and the teacher wants you to phone her."

"Anthony, you tell her for me that I work and run a house and that's her job, not mine. That's what she gets paid for, isn't it?"

Kim stood by Anthony and said, "Mum, we all have homework and someone has to help us."

"Fine, Kim. Ask Dad to help you. You can see how busy I am. I'm about to cook supper, do you want to eat or not? You can't have it both ways."

"Dad does help us when he can, but he's busy at work and doesn't get home until late a lot of the time."

As I sat at the kitchen table resting my chin in my hands, I stared through the open sliding door watching the beautiful golden corn blowing in the breeze. Anthony had gone out to play, leaving his homework on the counter. Robert had his hands in the cookie jar, and Kim had taken off to her room, upset with me.

Carolann, sensing I was upset, came up to me. "Mummy, you don't have to help me with my homework if it makes you sad."

How did my youngest child pick up on that? But sad wasn't the word for what I was feeling. The situation reminded me of the old wringer washer my mother had. I'd watch her put the sheets through the rollers, and the water would squeeze out. That's how my stomach felt when the kids talked of homework. It was a darkness no one could understand except those just like me who knew the fear of being found out. No! I could never tell my children I was illiterate. I was too ashamed. They'd get by. I knew they would. After all, I had managed... I was doing what was expected of me: I was a wife and mother, and I took good care of the house.

But if I really believed that, why was it always on my mind; why did I feel so sick inside?

"God, Andy, I feel so sick. It happens all the time now. Every damn time I eat."

"I told you weeks ago to go to the doctor's."

"I need a ride and you're at work all day."

"Damn it, Ellen, learn to bloody well drive!"

I looked at him. Why hasn't he figured it out yet? I can't read well enough to read the learner's manual. He must know something is wrong by now. Maybe he's ashamed of me. But then, maybe he doesn't know. Well, I'll never tell him. Then he might admit he's ashamed of me. I couldn't bear to hear him say it. He had a good education. How could he relate to me -so dumb! I hate myself! I hate myself for being so stupid! I never wanted it to be this way. I never chose this. And now it's coming back to haunt me as though I'd done it on purpose, and now I'm being punished all over again. And what of my children, my beautiful children? It's happening all over again. I can see it in their eyes, that same shame and fear. And it's my entire fault. I hate myself.

"Ellen, don't cry like that. I'm sorry, I didn't mean to snap your head off, and I'm just tired; make an appointment for tomorrow and I'll take you."

Andy put his arms around me while I sobbed for a long time. Poor Andy, he didn't have a clue why I was crying. Only God knew, but he'd turned his back on me forever. I had let the doctor kill my baby!

I had been feeling quite sick for several weeks, especially after eating. Apparently, from the test the doctor had done, I had a gallstone. As I packed my bags for the hospital, I worried about the ten days I'd miss at work. Then I thanked God for my friends who were willing to take care of the children. No Warren Farm for them. My mind flashed back to a time in Warren Farm when Sylvia had her face slapped because she talked while standing in line waiting to go to school. Miss Salad snatched her candies out of her hand. I waited at recess for her to come out to play so I could share some of mine with her, but they kept her in detention as well so I threw my candies in the dustbin. Thank God I had friends!

When Andy brought Kim up to the hospital the day before I was to go home, I knew immediately she was sick. Andy said she had a bad cold and would be fine. But the following day, when I arrived home and found Kim lying on the couch, I knew this was something more than flu. As we drove to the medical center, I held Kim in my arms. She was so lifeless. I was angry with Andy for not taking her before. But how could I say anything when he had been running back and forth to the hospital and visiting the children too.

"What do you mean; go into the hospital right away?" I asked. "Why does she have to go into the hospital right away? What's wrong with her?"

The doctor answered, "Without further tests I can't be sure, but I think her heart is in trouble."

Dear God, not again. Isn't it somebody else's turn? If you're punishing me, God, for what I've done, then punish me, but not my babies. What kind of a God are you that would punish innocent children for someone else's crimes? Maybe there isn't a God at all, and it's just one bloody big joke. If that's true, it's the cruelest joke that ever beset the human race. "You know what God? You're proof of how stupid I am. I question that you actually exist, yet talk to you all the time, asking you for favors knowing you're mad at me. Well! There's one consolation, if I'm a mistake, according to the Catholic faith, it's your fault because you made me!"

After some time in the hospital, Kim eventually made it home. Shortly after, I felt the depression creeping back, and I kept asking myself why? I thought about the time I'd spent away from the other children while in the hospital and then visiting Kim. So Andy and I went out to buy the children some toys, which we could not afford. But the happiness the boys showed on seeing their red bikes, Kim with her new clothes, and Carolann with her doll made it all worthwhile. The guilt and depression went away for a while.

The boys had two accidents on their bikes. The first was when Robert got a flat tire, and

Anthony decided to give him a ride on the back of his bike and pull Robert's along with his other hand. They rode down the main drag, on Trunk Road in Ladner, heavy with traffic. Anthony told the policemen, as he and Robert got into their car, that he was making a left hand signal, changed his mind and went right instead, and the car just hit the bike for no reason. The police were very nice and even brought the bike back. The only way they could get Robert to stop crying from the bump he took on his head was to let him play with the siren.

The other accident occurred when they were riding down the road full speed toward each other! The idea was to not be the first to chicken out. Unfortunately, they both took Victoria Crosses and had a head-on collision! Anthony came running into the house crying his little heart out. He told me he had cut his knee and would never forgive his brother for not helping him get up. As I picked Anthony up to comfort him, he went on to tell me that Robert just lay there and stared at him, not even offering to bring the bike home, which was still lying in the middle of the road.

A knock on the door revealed a neighbor with Robert in his arms. Robert was out cold! The bikes were banned for two weeks, a punishment which lasted two days. I was never very good at sticking to my words.

As our children fell farther and farther behind in school, I found myself trying to compensate every way I knew how. Anthony wanted a dog so we bought him a dachshund and named him Tasha. Everyone loved him, but he slept with Anthony. Carolann wanted some budgies, so we went out and bought two. Robert demanded goldfish and Anthony white mice. Kim found a white kitten out in the pouring rain, and like the typical mother hen she was, she had to nurse it back to health. Of course, then it never left!

Love for my children took precedence over all, eclipsing everything one would normally scream about. The dog had puppies, the cat had kittens and the mice quadrupled. Fear of my children feeling about me the way I once did about my mother helped me spend money I didn't have!

In a dysfunctional home, even the animals are affected. Returning from shopping one day, I found Andy, Kim, John and Caroline in the house, and all hell had broken loose. Kim had been cleaning out the birdcage when Tasha jumped up and ate one of the budgies. Caroline was trying to clean up the mess, but said the dog must have swallowed it whole because they could only find some ruffled feathers! John and Andy had to stifle their laughter. Unable to contain themselves, they took off outside. As though that wasn't bad enough, one week later Tasha ate one of the mice, and the kittens ate the gold fish. Blimey! What a carry on!

Sylvia was moving back to Canada, near me. Billy had remarried while in England to a girl named Pauline and was bringing her back to Canada to live. They all thought I had the flu, and that's the way Andy and I wanted it. The truth was I was falling apart at the seams, and suicide was on my mind more often than not. The psychiatrist I went to see put me on Valium and all I did was sleep. I knew sleeping could not solve my problem. However, being awake meant watching those I loved repeat an old cycle, and I knew the consequences would be unbearable.

The children were wonderful and tried to understand, but I could see the question in their eyes. Why was I crying so much?

And then one morning, darling Anthony wanted to cook me breakfast. Robert and Carolann hid under the kitchen table while Andy stood by the fire extinguisher! Kim was her usual self, trying to be helpful, so I wasn't surprised to see flowers on the tray. Oh! If only I could have drawn a picture of what took place next.

Anthony came into my bedroom, head held high, so proud of his accomplishment, Tasha right behind him as always. The others followed slowly. As Anthony was placing the tray of food upon my bed, his foot caught the corner of the rug. The eggs slid toward my bedspread, but Tasha caught them both in mid-air. Then he made a full charge toward the toast and ate it dead. Seeing the look on his master's face, Tasha realized he was 'dog meat'! He made a fast retreat between Carolann's legs, down the stairs toward the door. Thinking it was open Tasha, bashed his head on the glass sliding door.

His legs would have buckled under him, but his stomach, full from breakfast, was already on the ground. Crawling on all paws, head badly wounded stomach all swollen; he managed to find shelter under his master's bed.

Such laughter! It felt wonderful, all of us laughing together. Robert and Anthony held on to each other as the tears rolled down their faces, Robert's knees finally giving way to the floor. Just when the hilarity was fading, one of them would come up with some comment: "did you see how fast he went down those stairs; he slid on his stomach because his legs were too short." "Did you see how fast he ate those eggs, and he didn't even wait for the ketchup."

I'm sure we laughed for half an hour. For whatever reason, the laughter that day snapped me out of my depression. That day I threw the Valium down the toilet.

CHAPTER 12

Changing Tides

For a while, things seemed to go smoothly. I started going to night school to please Andy in hopes that he would see I cared. I was reading at a grade seven level. I was at a grade five level in other subjects; math was a disaster. It was agonizing, but I stuck it out until I completed grade seven in reading. Then I quit. Even though the teachers were very understanding, it seemed all too humiliating.

Then a friend offered me a part time job in an office. It was very simple work. I just had to copy dates out of one book into another. This meant permanent part-time and I could rely on the money, which I couldn't with picking mushrooms. Since it was only part-time, they didn't ask me for references or require an interview. Several months later, when they asked me if I would like to work full-time, I was terrified. They wanted me to operate the switchboard. As I heard myself saying, yes, I could hear that dark and all too familiar voice screaming: "Have you gone stark raving mad? You know you'll screw up. You couldn't run a switchboard to save your life. Try writing up a message, you idiot! You can't even spell. What in bloody hell do you think you're doing? You'll not only embarrass yourself when they fire you for incompetence, but what of the family?" I felt sick to my stomach.

Then there was the other, unfamiliar voice, very mixed up but supportive, saying, "If you don't give it a try it will mean you failed again. How will you look Andy in the face and what about the bills that are piling up?"

For the first six weeks of being on switchboard, I felt physically ill and lost fifteen pounds.

Andy was on my back about everything, or that's how it felt at the time. Probably I was feeling guilty for being so inadequate. Alcohol had become my only friend, the only thing that made me laugh anymore. People thought I was very funny when drinking, and I was always tops on everybody's party list. My heart told me there was a problem, but denial was what I knew best. I wasn't an alcoholic; that was absurd. I just had to learn to drink less. Andy was always asking me, "Do you have to drink so much?" I'd embarrassed him a few times.

One day after arriving home from work, Kim, who was now in grade eight, handed me a note from her teacher; she complained that I had not returned her phone calls and said, that it was important she speak to me regarding Kim's schoolwork. School reports were being sent home, but she would like to speak with me prior to sending Kim's.

Having used every reason under the sun to avoid seeing any of the children's teachers, I'd finally run out of excuses. Afraid to tell Andy about the number of phone calls there had been in the past, I decided to take my chances and see Kim's teacher.

"Mum, you're only going to a teacher's meeting not a fancy dress ball."

"Don't you want me to look respectable?"

"Of course I do, but you don't have to wear makeup and set your hair. Really, my teacher is very nice. And she won't bite you. Anyway, you don't have to dress up; everyone knows how pretty you are."

Pretty! That was a new word in my vocabulary. Andy had said many times I was beautiful, but I just figured that was what husbands were supposed to say to their wives. Not until Caroline said it to me one day after coming back from a party did I think it might be true. We had been out for the evening, and I had been dancing with a man when his wife took a jealous fit. That's when Caroline said, "I'm not surprised. You're a very good-looking woman."

When I got home that night, I ran upstairs to look into the mirror and was astonished to realize I didn't know the person staring back at me; pretty, yes, but a total stranger.

Kim was pleased I was at long last going to see her teacher because I'd changed my mind so many times before. Kim worried and fussed over everyone and was always trying to please me, although she was already doing far more than her share. She was very close to all her siblings, but I noticed she fussed over her brother Anthony more than the other two. We all worried about him. He looked so lost at times. He was now twelve and had become disinterested in school and only attended because we made him. He may have been a troubled child, but his friends always surrounded him. The phone would ring off the hook for him. One of my greatest concerns was he believed I did not love him, which was completely untrue; if only, he had not been neglected when he was small. Now I was paying the price and so was he.

Kissing Kim good-bye and leaving her to baby-sit, I walked to the school planning what to say to her teacher about never returning her phone calls or attending any meetings. All kinds of stories came to mind. So this is what it had come down to, making up stories. Lies! I stood on the sidewalk. Now I was a liar too! Come to think about it, most of my life had been a lie. Much of what I'd been taught was not true: now my children were inheriting the same lies.

The teacher was showing me Kim's book and discussing algebra. Algebra? I could barely pronounce the word. Being dressed up and making the most of my English accent, I figured she would never suspect I had no idea what she was talking about. Was algebra English or math?

Nodding my head politely, I explained how busy Kim's father and I had been; leading the teacher to believe I was appalled that Kim was so behind. I reassured her that Andy and I would work on it right away. She was very pleased and said she hoped from now on she would see more of me. Telling her she would, I left for home, vowing never to humiliate myself like that again.

I'm not sure when I first noticed Andy was coming home later than usual. He seemed to be drinking at odd hours. Seeing Andy depressed a lot of the time was also new to me. So one night I came right out and asked him to tell me what was wrong.

At first it was total denial, but I persisted, saying I'd noticed how upset he had seemed. He said he couldn't take the pressure of all the bills we had piled up.

Even as I was suggesting that we should sell the house, pay off the bills and start again, there was uneasiness I had no explanation for. Andy and I had always had lots of bills, and we managed to meet them. What most amazed me was his readiness to do as I had suggested.

The children were heartbroken we were selling the house. We tried explaining why, but knew it was impossible for them to understand they were losing their home because their parents were irresponsible. And that was the truth. It need never have happened. I often bought things to cheer myself up. The next day I'd feel guilty for spending the money and told myself I wasn't worthy of new things.

The house we had lived in for almost seven years was gone, sold within six weeks. I felt numb.

We rented a house on Steveston Highway in Richmond. Busy trying to get the house in order and holding down a full time job, I wasn't immediately aware that nothing had changed with Andy. Four weeks had passed since we had moved in, and Christmas was on my mind. While trying to make plans, I realized Andy was never around to talk to. He was still coming home late.

One night I waited up for him. It was well past three in the morning when he arrived home. He began to make excuses about Christmas coming up and the boys asking him out for a drink. Andy had never gone out without me before. The thought of other women crossed my mind, but that was ridiculous. He would never do that to me. Besides, I'd know if he was. Many women claimed they didn't know, but I always thought that was a lie. They just didn't want to deal with it. No! That thought was silly.

"Andy this has got to stop. Please tell me what's wrong. We sold the house so all our problems would go away, but you're still depressed. Please, for once in your life speak to me."

"It's my job. It has become too much, and I'm overloaded with work. Just give me some time, and it will sort itself out."

"What are you talking about, Andy? Listen to yourself! You told me it was because of the debts. Andy, we sold the house to make you happy, and now it's something else! Have you gone mad? Do you know what it cost this family to move? The kids were heartbroken when they had to change schools!"

Then the most unspeakable hideous truth hit me. How stupid! How incredibly stupid I'd been; so bloody naive. Dear God, this wasn't happening to me. Andy was in love with another woman!

Falling into the chair, I stared across at the man I'd lived with for nearly sixteen and half years. He was a total stranger. We had four children together. Surely we knew each other?

At first, when I accused him of it, he denied it. But even as he did, the look on my face told him denial was pointless. Six people's lives would never be the same again, all because of a woman. Worst of all, that woman was me.

My insecurities had driven him away. There had been little conversation. Depressions I didn't understand. I often ran to my sister Ann, instead of sharing with Andy or trying to think for myself. I was afraid of people. I drank too much, spent money we didn't have, feared going inside a bank, never learned to drive, missed parent-teacher meetings and relied on Andy to take us everywhere. I couldn't even grocery shop without him because I barely had a grade seven education. I couldn't get a job with better pay.

My thoughts rushed back to my mother saying to me, "You were a mistake; two children were enough." Not only had I failed by being born, but now I had also failed the only purpose to my entire life: marriage!

Some would disagree and say some of the blame lay with Andy. He too carried unwanted pain from his childhood. The only thing we had in common was that neither of us knew how to deal with our hurt. We had come to believe pain and frustration was our lot in life. Why didn't it just go away? There had been prayers born of desperation, but with no real belief in them. My faith had deserted me a long time ago. With no real discussion about reconciliation, or consideration of how badly the children might be hurt, Andy and I decided to get a divorce.

Andy sat in silence as I told Kim and Carolann what was happening. Kim never said what she felt; she went off into her room. Carolann seemed confused. Her only concern was would she be living with me? Reassuring her she would, she went outside to play. Then we called the boys together and told them. Robert was very angry and turned toward me screaming. He told me to fix it. He seemed to think it was like when his bike had a flat tire, and I picked him up when he hurt himself. He begged me to tell dad I was sorry. For what, he did not know. As for Anthony, he laughed, saying this is a joke, right? He said, "You and Dad never even argue, why you would split up?" There was silence for a while, and then Anthony said, "It's my fault, isn't it Mum because I'm always in trouble."

No matter what I said, he walked out believing the fault was all his.

CHAPTER 13

Tunnel Of Darkness

By October of 1979, I was divorced. It astonished me how seventeen years of marriage was over, gone, almost as though they had never been. Was this the fashion, the 'in' thing? What of our children, their shattered lives? What had they learned from it all? That nothing is sacred anymore; marriage is a farce? To run when the going gets tough? I love you, but.

Being enveloped in shame and self-pity, I hardly noticed how Kim had quietly taken over as caregiver. I cried a lot, terrified as to how I'd cope without Andy and Caroline. John and Caroline had moved to the states, I'd lost the one friend who believed in me. Kim, now sixteen took over the household and chores and kept reassuring me all would be fine.

Learning to drive had me craving the cigarettes I'd given up a few years back. There was no way I wanted to learn to drive, but there was no longer a choice. Without Andy, I had to be able to get to work. What if there was an emergency with the children and he wasn't around?

I went over the learner's manual for three months before understanding it. I wondered if there were other people out there driving around who couldn't read very well either. Just reading the bloody manual was bad enough; trying to comprehend what it meant drove me crazy. Getting my learner's permit was another nerve-racking experience. By March 1980, at almost forty years old, I had my license and was driving myself to work. Despite feeling extremely nervous, there was a sense of accomplishment. I had the overwhelming urge to roll down the window and yell to passersby, "Look at me driving." Actually, I did do it once in the car, to myself!

I was so thankful for my sister Sylvia. Still not married, she seemed to spend her life taking care of other people, especially when they were in need. She would constantly phone to check up on me or invite me over to supper and include me on her long walks beside the water, knowing it was my favorite place.

Ann phoned me from Montreal when she heard about my divorce. She urged me to take God into my life, a suggestion Sylvia seconded. I was infuriated but didn't say so. "To hell with God," I had decided. I was going to start having a good time and forget about all that crap. When a guy at work asked me out on a date, I went. My philosophy was to take one dreaded day at a time. Never stopping to worry about what the children were doing, I went out every weekend drinking and occasionally smoking dope. My only worry was working on Mondays with a hangover.

I had decided the boys should live with Andy and the girls live with me. Since I was now working full time and living on my own, I was afraid to take on all four. I felt incapable. Anthony, now thirteen, was skipping school a great deal, causing chaos with his father. Robert looked up to Anthony, often doing as he did. Kim was working very hard to complete her last year of high school, while trying to keep the peace between her father and brothers. Carolann rarely brought home any schoolwork. When she did, I made a point of not asking her about it. She was a very quiet child and stayed in her room for much of the time. I saw nothing unusual about that. Wasn't it what I always did when I was her age?

Andy and I spoke often because we were worried about the children. However, we always seemed to talk in circles and never really accomplished anything. We had taken Anthony to a psychiatrist; put him in an alternative school, but to no avail.

Early one July morning while driving to work, my brakes failed. Jamming the brake pedal down as far as it would go; I smashed into the back of the car in front of me. My knees hit the dashboard, my face collided with the steering wheel and for a few seconds everything went black. Through the blood pouring from my face, I looked down at my left ankle; it was bent to one side and swollen.

Naturally, Sylvia was by my bedside in the hospital within minutes, and only then did I begin to cry. My nose was cracked, my ankle was badly sprained and both my knees were swollen up. My seat belt had left a welt on my neck. My face was horribly distorted from all the swelling.

My car was totaled. The feeling of being a loser was growing again.

It was two weeks before I was able to return to work, and when I did, they fired me! Just like that. Fired after three and half years; once again, because I did not know how to stand up for myself and figured it must have been my fault, I just accepted it.

Fear! Why was I still so afraid? Fear was making me sick and weak in my stomach. I was out of work and couldn't imagine who would hire me. I hadn't had an interview in years. Searching through the papers day in and day out, going from one interview to another, I finally landed a job as a switchboard receptionist for a stockbroker. The pay was low but it was a job.

I eventually found another job with much better pay at another company. I had worked so hard at the interview to get the job. I was exquisitely dressed, my hair immaculate. I emphasized my accent and carried one of Ayn Rand's books, having seen the movie "Fountain Head" based on the novel by Ayn Rand! I thought I'd fooled them all. But I had fooled only myself. Seeing only the money, I accepted the position, only to be fired four months later for incompetence. My poor messaged-writing and spelling were impossible to hide.

Welfare! I couldn't believe I'd sunk so low.

When Kim came knocking on the door a few weeks later, she found me crying. She had graduated and was doing an apprenticeship in hairdressing. She suggested we pack up and move elsewhere and start all over again. She felt if I got away I might feel better about finding a job.

When Kim mentioned Vancouver Island, my favorite place, there was no thinking twice. Carolann was unhappy about the move because it meant changing her friends and schools again. I overlooked the ever-increasing silence that was taking over her life. She reminded me of a beautiful seashell, only I failed to see how deep she was digging into the sand. The thought of leaving the boys behind was too painful to consider, so I ignored it.

Making a change, any change, was easier than thinking things out. Whenever I tried that, it made me feel nauseated, and then I always wanted a drink. Making a move like this was bound to make me feel better, and then I'd stop drinking. After all, I didn't really enjoy alcohol. In fact, I hated the taste of booze. I knew I'd quit once I settled down into a new life. But I had to get my priorities straight first. I had to find a job.

Billy and Pauline ran a motel in Victoria and offered Kim and me a room until we found a place of our own. Andy had moved again and had to give up Tasha. If I had not been such a coward, I might have phoned and talked to Anthony, knowing he must have been heartbroken. Kim and Carolann said the boys weren't doing too well and were getting into all kinds of trouble, so my phone calls to them became fewer because hearing the truth might make me want to have them with me. That would have meant more responsibility and would mean I couldn't go out in the evening as often as I did. Leaving Carolann home on her own was all right because she was quiet, but having the responsibility of two boys might put a damper on my nights out on the town.

Friday and Saturday nights were all I lived for. We had become regulars at the same bar, Billy, Pauline, Kim and I. Kim never drank much. But I felt my role was to drink until I was happy! Occasionally, I'd wake up in the morning and remember something funny from the night before. Like the time Billy had put his back out. So bad was his back that he could hardly walk. Now this was very serious because it meant he couldn't walk down to the pub. But that didn't deter Pauline and me! We phoned the Red Cross and borrowed a wheelchair.

Getting to the pub was no problem; it was downhill. But getting home was something else. First of all we had to push two hundred and fifty pound Billy up the hill. On top of that, Pauline and I were highly intoxicated. Billy objected to our lack of control, especially when we accidentally let go and he rolled backwards into the oncoming traffic. Yelling at him as he rolled backwards, we reassured him the wheels would probably catch the bumper of the cars, and push him back up the hill. We were laughing hysterically, but Billy screamed so loudly, we had to run after the wheelchair and start pushing it back up the hill. He called us female dogs and other obscene things, but we paid no attention. I was much more interested in Pauline showing me how she could walk without her polio limp. Pauline had walked with a limp since she was two years old.

"Shut your gob, Bill!" she yelled, "I'm showing Ellen something. Now watch me, Ellen, when I walk with one foot on the sidewalk and one foot in the road. See? I walk normal."

"Watch me Pauline!" I cried, "I can do that and walk like you normally do. Now! What's wrong with Billy?"

"Ignore him Ellen. If he wants to be childish and walk the rest of the way home, fine. Come on, get in the wheelchair and I'll give you a ride home."

My drinking had become a pick-me-up, a get-me-through-the-evening and a put-me-to-sleep. I had the Dial-A-Bottle number in the liquor cabinet, hidden behind the tall glasses. Frightened of what was happening to me, I kept telling myself I'm just going through a bad phase. It'll pass.

When Robert phoned one day to ask if he could come and live with me, I was surprised and pleased. Now it meant Carolann wouldn't be so lonely, and she'd have someone to go to school with. At least that's what I thought!

Although Robert did end up being company for Carolann, they constantly skipped out of school. Some weeks passed before I noticed that Robert wasn't even interested in leaving the house. In fact, he lay on the couch hardly getting up except to eat. His mood had utterly changed. Where once he filled the house with laughter, he now filled it with anger. No one could speak to him without him snapping back. Robert had become unbearable to talk to, and he slept all the time. How could anyone sleep so much?

I reflected back to a dark and lonely place where I had been at Robert's age. Hadn't I too wanted the world to stop and let me off? No! This wasn't going to happen to my Robert! I grieved for him then as I had when Carolann had nearly died of pneumonia. I grieved for his tortured mind, and his soul, lost somewhere in the bleakness of his life.

Robert was opposed to seeing a psychologist, and the suggestion made him even angrier with me. When the doctor found Robert had ulcers, in addition to his depressed mental state, he suggested putting him into the hospital in the children's' ward on a five-week program. Kim, Carolann, and I swore one another to secrecy. No one outside of our immediate family was to know he was in the Eric Martin Institute for the mentally ill. All too well I remembered back in England you were never allowed to associate with someone who had a mental illness. It was all right for the body to break down but not the mind, that wasn't allowed to get sick.

In desperation, I went to Saint Andrew's Cathedral to talk to a priest. It had been a long time since I had gone into a church, but I felt at a loss as to where to turn. There was certainly nothing to lose. Father Charles hadn't actually been ordained yet but would be within the year. He visited Robert, and they quickly became friends.

Charles invited me to his ordination. Never having been to one before, I accepted. The church was packed, and I couldn't sit where I had hoped and ended up sitting on the far outside. Who knows why certain things happen, perhaps only God is meant to know, but Charles came out of the very door next to where I was seated. As the procession came by, he made a point of smiling at me, touching my arm as he walked by.

It was the most spiritual service I'd ever attended. I was filled with a peace I had never thought possible. On leaving the church, the peace left me. But whatever transpired during that service, I knew my life would never be the same.

At the same time, the fear of having to change was overwhelming. Me! Change? I figured I would have changed by now if it had been possible. Since that service, I began to sneak into church and sit at the back. It was as though I was afraid someone might see me and think I'd gone religious.

One day while sitting in church with a bloody great hangover, I asked Our Lady in prayer about abortion, begging her to help me understand whether it was right or wrong. I explained to Mary how my mother had suffered because she had too many children and didn't know how to cope, and her children suffered as a result. My own parenting was even worse. I was a rotten mother! So wasn't the child I aborted better off? Was it really murder? I didn't understand why I was so concerned about this after so many years. Tears rolled down my face. I held my head in my hands and I wept.

What took place next was, in my mind, a miracle. While asking Mary for help, I felt a gentle hand on my shoulder. Startled, I found myself looking up into the face of a very tall man. He had the most incredible pale blue eyes that seemed to sparkle, and on his serene face was a smile just as wonderful. His grey hair hung way down his back and his beard was just as long. He was wearing a pair of jeans and a three quarter length coat, similar to that of a merchant seaman's. Still with an angelic smile on his face, he put a picture of Our Lady in my hand and, without ever speaking, walked away. I read on the back: *Jesus, Mary and Joseph, I love you very much, I beg you to spare the life of the unborn baby that I have spiritually adopted who is in danger of abortion. During your earthly life this spiritually adopted child of yours will be known only to God, but in the world*

*to come and throughout eternity both you and the child
will find happiness in each other's company.*

As I sat there crying for a long time, I came to
realize how much my children really meant to me.
Even though two of them had not been in my plans,
I understood in God's eyes they were. For the first
time I was clearly aware of how glad I was to have
had four. They were all so different: Kim, the
caregiver; Anthony, strong headed with a heart of
gold; Robert, the comedian; Carolann, the quiet one,
the treasured listener. Each had completely different
personalities and needs. "How do I love thee? Let
me count the ways." I loved my children dearly.

Eventually, Robert joined Charles,
catechumen class to receive his first communion and
be confirmed into the Roman Catholic faith.
Carolann's despondency worried me so much that I
let her go and live with her father, hoping she would
rejoin her friends and stay in school. The fear of her
ending up in Robert's situation was more than I
could bear.

One morning I woke up with a heavy
hangover and crawled into the kitchen. Kim was
standing at the sink washing dishes. The silence
between us was a troubled emptiness.

"Mum, we have to talk."

"Not now Kim. Can't you see I'm coming
down with the flu?"

"No mother, we have to talk now. Last night
was the last straw. I can't take your drinking. I had
to stay up all night and take care of you because I
was afraid you would roll on to your back in the
night and choke. You threw up from one end of the
house to the other, and I had to clean it up. If you
don't quit drinking, I'm leaving and finding a place
of my own."

Dear Lord, wasn't there something wrong
with this scene? Wasn't it usually parents who
threaten the kids to behave?

That same day, Kim took me to a religious
bookstore to buy something. She was really back
into her faith, and I was truly pleased about that.
While waiting for her to purchase a book, I browsed

through the store and the words of a poem jumped out at me. It was "Footprints In The Sand." Those words went over and over in my mind a thousand times, the part where it read, "when you saw only one set of footprints in the sand, it was then that I was carrying you."

I ran out, leaned up against the wall and cried. Everyone was looking at me, but the tears just kept on coming. Poor Kim was so embarrassed, and there was no explanation to give her because I didn't understand myself. Why doesn't He leave me alone? God, I don't bother you! Why are you hunting me down? What do you want of me? I'm illiterate. I'm a drunk and on welfare. I can't be of any use to you, leave me alone!

Kim took me home, but the ugliness of my life was about to become more ugly. We'd been inside the door five minutes when the phone rang. Robert was on the other end. He and Carolann had gone to Vancouver to help their Dad move. He was all upset because while carrying a box of Carolann's things he had dropped it and all her papers fell out. A letter

Carolann had written a few weeks earlier caught his eye. He was shocked to read she had taken cocaine and a powerful drug called lysergic acid diethylamide, LSD. I felt immediate denial. Robert doesn't read that well. But the knowing scream in my head told me otherwise and accused me of having seen it coming for a long time. Hanging up the phone, I walked into the living room as though my feet where made of lead. As I sank onto my green couch, hardly able to breathe, I had a flash back of a time when a teacher had asked me to come to the front of the class and work out a math problem on the black board. I couldn't and he hit me. There was no escape as he blocked the door, feeling trapped I began struggling to breathe. I was so afraid, and I knew I had to find a way to figure it out.

My children were trapped in a desolate tunnel, the walls wet with their tears, no windows for them to see out of, no doors for them to escape through. The bricks were breaking away, rotting from the dampness, coming loose one by one, falling

to strike their already broken hands.   Still they
stumbled along struggling toward the light, hoping
to escape.

What had I done? What in hell's name had I
done? Nothing. Absolutely nothing. I could hear
the ticking of the clock on the living room wall. I
wanted to get up and smash it to pieces, to stop time,
to turn it back, but the hands continued to move
forward without me.

CHAPTER 14

Love On The Rocks

Looking across the table in the restaurant at Kim, I wondered if she loved me and, if so, why? Kim had grown up long before her time, never experiencing the life a teenager might have. I looked at her still angelic face, her big almond eyes, but saw lines of worry.

My children were the only sparks left within me, and I had failed them miserably. I looked at the menu, and having difficulty in reading it, I thought of Anthony; tall, handsome, brown hair, dark eyes, all the girls chasing after him. He had dropped out, in grade eight. Living with his friends, he was running completely wild. As much as I try to reach him, he pulls farther and farther away. The waitress interrupted my thoughts; I ordered a glass of wine and, not being able to read the menu, said I'd have what Kim's having.

As Kim talked to me about wanting to attend Camosun College to get her Early Childhood Education, my thoughts went to Robert having failed two grades. How much humiliation could a child take? I knew it was just a matter of time before he quit too. His hair was black like my mother's and his eyes just as dark. Still, with his round baby face and the smile to go with it, he seemed to hold his own. Every one loved Robert, the gentle giant. His best friend was his brother, and they couldn't have been more opposite. Anthony, with his long hair and tattoos, was always in some sort of a brawl, and Robert, with his short hair and gentle ways, was always trying to calm him down. The waitress brought our food to the table and Kim talked for a while on how she would find the

Money, to go to college; I thought college was for the rich.

As I sipped my wine, I reflected upon Carolann and as young as Carolann was, she already had the guys' heads turning, and I was glad she was the quiet type. She was striking, tall, thin, with long black hair, an oval shaped face, and dark eyes and full lips. I saw great potential in her and hoped one day she would heal enough that she might pursue her dreams, whatever they may be. She was still battling it out at school after failing grade nine, but we managed to sort some things out. I felt good that she was seeing a psychiatrist. I still couldn't believe the police found out she was getting her drugs from a prison inmate on a weekend pass.

Kim was saying something. "Earth to mother, you haven't heard one word I've said."

"Kim, do you love me?"

"That is a ridiculous question. Whatever made you ask me that?"

"I've been a rotten mother to you kids. And I can see how it has affected each one of you and the struggles you are going through as a result."

"Mum, you've never been a rotten mother, and we all love you very much, but your drinking this past year isn't funny like it used to be. Instead of waiting up for you to come home, we run to our bedrooms pretending we're asleep."

"Anthony hates me, Kim. I can feel it."

"No he doesn't. He's angry with you, and there's a difference. You may have let us down, but worse you let yourself down. If only I could get you to see, Mum, you have great potential and could do so much more with your life."

"Don't you think I'd like to believe that? Do you think I like what I've become, nothing but a bum on social assistance."

"Go out and find a job."

"Don't be foolish, who's going to hire someone that barely has grade ten, can't count or spell to save her life?"

"Try going back to school."

"I tried that, remember?"

"Two things you're forgetting about, Mother. One, you have a drinking problem, and two, you became very sick. From that time you just seemed to give up. But you know what sticks in my mind the most? When you did go, you enjoyed it. Doesn't that tell you something? Mum, your drinking has to stop. If it doesn't, you'll lose us."

Some of Kim's words kept running around in my head, "you'll lose us" and "where will it all end?" Lose the only reason I had left for living, my children?

Looking down at my half finished glass of red wine, I asked Kim if she wanted to finish it. She declined and as we left the restaurant, I glanced back over my shoulder at the unfinished wine, never imagining it would be my last drink.

Six months later, I went to my first Alcoholics Anonymous meeting. It was awful. I believed going into A.A. was scraping the bottom of the barrel. The idea that it might be a major turning point in my life was inconceivable. My sobriety was white-knuckled. It was like losing a close friend. No one to turn to, to see me through the evenings, help me to sleep at nights, get me through the rough times.

The children had always taken second place. There was no way of turning the clock back and there was no way of knowing if they would give me a second chance at being a mother. But I was determined to give it all I had. How could I ever manage to do that?

For almost a year I had been seeing a psychiatrist, Dr. Lawrence Pazdar. When I look back now I don't know what I would have done without him. He saw me through some of the roughest times of my life. He encouraged me to talk about the past and see clearly how it had affected my life.

At times it was so painful that I wondered if it were worth going back to see him, but I had to get rid of the garbage once and for all. He helped me realize that it wasn't all in my head, and I wasn't doing a 'poor me'. Most important of all, just because I was brought up in the same family didn't mean my feelings should be the same as my siblings. After all, we were all treated differently according to my parents' likes and dislikes. One of the most perilous things I discovered about dysfunctional families, mine included, is the suppression, being told '"don't talk about it, it's a secret," it's over now, you'll soon forget", "It wasn't that bad!", or better yet "you asked for it!"

The best way to shut me up was to tell me of someone worse off than me, like when Mum told me about all the Jews in the holocaust. That left me with a great sense of guilt and the feeling it must all be in my head, reinforcing how stupid I was. So I had repressed my feelings for years, letting nightmares tear me apart. Sometimes I was afraid to go to sleep at night. There were many things I didn't understand about my childhood, but what I learned to laugh about now were the "secrets," that everybody knew about.

Christmas was coming. Kim and I made wonderful plans. She had moved out and was living with her boyfriend. Robert and Carolann had both moved back with their father in hopes that they would stay in school being with their old friends and familiar surroundings. Anthony was living with his girlfriend and planned to spend time with us too. We were all excited about the idea of being together. We never dreamed that by Christmas Eve we'd all be in shock.

Carolann announced she was pregnant!

My shy, quiet one. Thoughts flashed through my mind in rapid-fire sequence. How could this happen? It's my entire fault. I'll kill him. Then, as my thoughts began to slow down, I wondered, does she want the baby or an abortion? If she does give birth, will she keep it or give it up for adoption?

Even before Carolann had told me of her plans, I had already made up my mind to tell her if she didn't want the baby, I would adopt it. What if she wants to keep it? How could she manage to be a mother at seventeen when I couldn't manage in my forties?

Too many unanswered questions. That was the most I'd craved a drink in two years and nine months.

CHAPTER 15

Banished Children of Eve

While on the phone to my friend Diana, whom I'd met at church, I told her all that had happened and asked her what was going to happen to me? And how would I be able to handle all of this? Gently, she asked me if perhaps it might be Carolann who should be asking the questions, and I might just try giving her all the support she would obviously need. During this conversation she also suggested that I might take a three-day workshop in January for recovering alcoholics. I thought it rather a stupid idea since I had been sober so long. But she said something about my attitude, and that maybe spending time with other people like myself, I might have a better understanding of my thoughts and feelings.

As it turned out, Carolann was determined to bring her own baby up with the help of its father.

With the beginning of a new year our lives were once again changing. The three-day workshop, my friend Diana had encouraged me to go to would be coming to an end and I was anxious to go home. My feelings of anger were so great that I was sorry I'd ever consented to coming in the first place. The idea of being here was to feel better. So why was I hurting so much, as I had so many times after leaving Dr. Pazder's office?

One of the counselors told me I was a walking time bomb and would do one of two things, go back to drinking or try committing suicide. She said she was amazed with the anger I was carrying around that I'd stayed sober this long. As I got up to leave, not wanting to listen to any more of her negativity, she said something that shocked me.

"Ellen, you have great potential because you have an enormous capacity to love; there's great power in that, but you fail in an area that destroys many lives. You don't love yourself."

I stopped. "Isn't that rather vain: to love yourself?"

"Is that what you believe, to love yourself is wrong? Think, Ellen! Who do you spend most of your life with? Who looks after your thoughts and feelings, your pain? Who looks after the love, the dreams, the joy and sorrow? Give it some thought, Ellen; and while you're doing that remember, you own all that baggage we talked about these past three days. You have to get rid of that before you can feel any real love for yourself."

She paused, her eyes searching, "I think it would be a really good idea for you to come back and stay for a month, here at the treatment center. I truly believe you would find it very beneficial, but it has to be your choice. Whatever you decide, don't look back at the past. Look at the present and what you have accomplished. Ellen, did you ever believe you would be sober for nearly three years? You achieved that on your own. Don't lose it! You're worthwhile."

Worthwhile! What did she mean? Me! How in the blazes does someone love themselves? A great capacity to love! I still wasn't sure what love really meant. Thoughts raced around in my head but one stood out. If there was someone I didn't like, I avoided that person. Is that what I'd been doing all my life, avoiding myself?

One Sunday, in the spring of 1987, I went to mass. The need to go was so intense, as if it was my last chance.

Then I made my way to spend a month at a treatment center on Dallas Road in Victoria. As I walked up the path, suitcase in hand, I felt as though I was going to my own funeral. I felt deep shame. How could it ever have come to this? I heard the voice of my dragon coming from out of the darkness, "You've been sober almost three years, and you don't belong here." Then there was the other voice, the one that had started to speak up more often, "What have you got to lose? Who knows what you might gain? If all else fails, think about this: Do you want this sick feeling in the pit of your stomach for the rest of your life?"

The house reminded me of an old type cottage I'd once seen in England. Standing on the front porch, the wind picked up, carrying a strong scent of the sea air. It seemed to wrap protectively around me. Out of my past came two memories: myself as a little girl happily picking daisies with my sister and as a desperate young teenager standing at the edge of the pier. I had a sudden compulsion to cry. Whatever made me think of those things now? It was bewildering, wanting to cry for those memories. I'd never wanted to cry about the past before. Had I, and why now? I was forty-five years old!

"Hello, my name's Randy, I'm one of the counselors. What might your name be?"

I wanted to say "the forty-five year-old idiot," but refrained. I shook his hand and introduced myself. He asked me to sit down so we could have a chat before he showed me around and took me to meet the others. Some had arrived that day, others a couple of days earlier. There were to be twelve of us altogether. In our first week we were not allowed phone calls, and we couldn't go outside for the first few days.

As Randy introduced me to the others, I might have laughed if it hadn't been so tragic. Some of us were dressed to the nines, while others were barely hanging on to what they were wearing. We were from all walks of life, different faiths, cultures and orientations, off the street, from the best of homes, government officials and welfare recipients. Some were well educated and others illiterate. This was the most mixed bag of people with whom I'd ever come in contact.

I was shown to my room upstairs, which I would be sharing with two other women. The room was square with two windows on one side of the room, each with a bed underneath and another overlooking the ocean, that's where mine was. I sat on my bed for a while and wondered what the two girls would be like and would they like me? Who had slept here before me with shattered lives? What hopes and dreams did they have, and had this place helped turn their world around? I hated the thought of going back down the stairs to meet the rest of the people. I was afraid of what they would think of me; an illiterate, white-knuckled sobriety, single mother of four on welfare who couldn't get her life together. I was filled with shame, guilt and self-loathing. I particularly didn't like the idea of them thinking I had failed my children.

Forcing myself down the stairs, I was met halfway by Randy coming up with a young man who had arrived late. He was introduced to me as George, but I would come to know him as Kelly. Shaking his hand, I noticed his pitifully thin body, his clothes hanging on his back. He had small, pale blue eyes and long blond hair, a black eye and a broken jaw. But his broken face was less tragic than the evidence of his wounded life so clearly imprinted upon his face. It was disturbing. I felt as though if I reached out and touched his face, I'd physically feel his pain. He said "Hello," softly and then continued his way up to find his room.

After a restless night, I made my way down to the dining room. There we were twelve of us sitting around the table staring at each other. Although we were total strangers, we had one thing in common: the light in our lives had gone out. For some of us, it had never been lit.

Every morning we all gathered in one room. After a few days, we started to share more deeply of our misery and bitterness. Everyone was filled with anguish and torment from the oldest to the youngest. Many times we would cry along with the person telling the story or get angry with the person who had inflicted the pain. There had been sexual and physical abuse, alcoholism, drugs and emotional turmoil. Some of us were from strong religious backgrounds, while others hated the very idea. Some felt loved; most of us did not. Many of us had been tainted in early childhood. And although some of those who had imposed the grief upon us had died or moved away, our wounds had not gone with them. The wounds festered, as though determined to devour any hopes or dreams we once might have had. Why did the sores not heal with the departure of the disease? Why did certain readings from the

Bible keep coming to my mind? 'Weep not for me but for your children, Christ said to the women as he carried his cross.' Or in the Old Testament 'The sins of the Fathers shall fall upon thy children.' Sometimes we laughed, realizing that some of us had become the very people we despised most.

One morning during a session, I shared how much I'd loved the beach as a child, how it was my sanctuary. Yet I also felt a sadness because I'd seen other parents playing with their children while mine had been nowhere around. What touched me most was watching parents help their children build sandcastles. I wanted to build one so badly, but always a feeling of inadequacy overcame me. Afraid my castle would look silly in comparison to the others around me, I wouldn't attempt it. I realized my face was wet, and began apologizing to the group for getting emotional about a pile of sand. Perhaps I wouldn't have lost control if there had not been so many streaming faces around me. And so the sobbing began. Tears burst forth as though they had been trying to escape for years.

That afternoon, the counselors gave us a project. We were to go down to the beach and help Ellen Blanche Challand Szita build a sandcastle! So there we all were, down on our hands and knees helping this grandmother-to-be finally build her first castle. I looked up into the face of my roommate, my eyes still swollen from crying. I saw a beautiful Jewish woman smiling down at me. "Ellen, this is your entire fault. There's sand in my hair and inside my shoes."

Laughing, I continued to build my sand castle. It felt wonderful, and for a precious moment, I was the little girl I'd always wanted to be.

Looking around me, tears welled up in my eyes. There was a young man trying to break his cocaine habit. There was a young First Nations mother of three, trying to stay sober so she might hold onto the children she loved so much. To my left was a handsome young First Nations fellow, whom I'll call, Peter: a brilliant carver who wanted sobriety so he could earn a living with his ingenious hands. Another man, beside Peter, confessed to us he thought alcoholics were disgusting and that cocaine, an expensive habit, at least gave him some dignity.

Then there was Kelly. Kelly had a gift few human beings had: the ability to give and love expecting nothing in return.

One evening, after several weeks at the center, I went down to the basement to wash my clothes. It had cement walls with no windows with a small light bulb above the washing machine. It was one of those places I'd constantly keep looking out for spiders or someone ready to jump out at me. So I was glad to see Kelly come down with Peter to do laundry too.

Kelly was in his thirties. He was trying to stay sober, but admitted he had been in and out of detox for some years. The three of us sat talking until well after midnight. By then, I had mended all tears in their clothes and ironed them as well. During that time, we shared more between us than we had in the entire previous month.

The whole time Kelly talked, he twisted his hair around his finger as a child might do. Peter sat crossed-legged on the floor carving a bird. He told us he was afraid to go back to the reservation because so many of his people drank. Yet they were his family, and he loved them.

"Ellen, what are you most afraid of?" Peter asked.

"Changing. Changing might make me feel lonelier than I do already."

"Explain that to me."

I picked up the iron, now gone cold, and began wrapping it with the old brown cord. I then proceeded to fold our laundry, putting it into individual piles, and went on to answer Peter's question.

"For me to change is to go into an unknown world, to break away from all that's familiar. When I became sober I felt like I'd lost a friend, becoming lonelier than ever before. Yet alcohol really wasn't my friend; in fact, it was destroying me."

Having finished folding up the laundry, I put the iron away in the cupboard and leaned up against the chipped sink and the old brown arborite counter.

"Nevertheless," I continued, "when I drank I knew what to expect: hangover, guilt, being short of rent or food money, strange looks from the children, silence that slapped me in the face, feeling ill and blaming it on the flu -which no one believed anymore."

"I'm even afraid to think for myself; I've always let others do it for me. There were many times I didn't agree with someone but felt at a loss for the right words, so rather than make a fool of myself, I just pretended to agree and hated every moment of it. It made me feel cowardly. All my life I've felt incapable of making decisions. When I was a child, no matter what conclusion I came to, it was never the right one. Then there's the crippling pain and hate from the past. That has become the center of my being, never allowing me to trust anything unfamiliar. When I think back, I realized I learned very young not to trust anyone. I built a protective wall around myself. Now I'm starting to a see that's what's held me back. Still, the thought of tearing it down fills me with dread. You know, you guys, I know this sounds crazy, and it is, but I'm so fed up with being afraid of fear."

Peter spoke, "We three have something in common, fear of the unknown, starting with ourselves! Fear to walk outside the door at the end of the month because for us to change means stepping into an alien world. What do you think, Kelly? Say something; you've gone quiet."

"Actually, I was thinking about something."

"Kelly," I teased, "you should know by now, it's dangerous for us alcoholics to think. I'm reporting you to the staff in the morning."

Kelly looked at us both. "Seriously, since age fourteen I haven't been sober more than a few weeks, and I want so badly to stay dry. The only reason I'm here," Kelly hesitated, "is because I've been thinking about suicide. The craving for a drink is like a fire burning my insides. I feel physical pain.

Then I try to fix that with dope and then other things. And then I'm back in detox."

Hearing a snap, I looked over at Peter just in time to see the head of his partially carved bird roll along the floor. Peter's knuckles were as white as his face. It left me wondering what had gone through his mind.

As the three of us silently climbed the stairs, I noticed we were all looking down at the basement floor at the partially carved head of what I realized was an eagle. What were we all thinking as we stared down at it? Afraid that's how we might end up, broken, never to see the daylight? Dying in the darkness, never to go beyond the cement walls?

The following morning Kelly and I went to mass, and I prayed that our roads of suffering would become a highway to glory for all of us. It was time to move on and take a chance. They say, "Time waits for no man." Time waits for no future grandma either!

Finally the day came for us to leave. I was apprehensive. When we hugged each other good-bye, the affection was real. We knew the month we had spent together would never be forgotten. Peter hugged me tight, and said something so wonderful it remained forever in my treasured memories. He told me, if he ever had a chance to pick a mother, he'd choose me. As I watched my handsome friend walk out the door with tears in his eyes, I yelled out to him, "Remember, you're the roots to this country. Be proud!"

As for Kelly, I took him home with me, like a lost puppy found outside in the pouring rain. This ran counter to the advice we had been given when leaving the center, not to get into any relationships for one year.

For the first few days after I got back home, I kept thinking about my mother. The memories seemed triggered by Carolann's pregnancy and made me wonder how my mother ever managed seven pregnancies on her own, especially with dad away most of the time in the navy. I realized how lonely and frightened my mother must have been. I was glad Carolann was going to have the support of the baby's father.

All the things I knew of Mum, her suffering throughout her lifetime, seemed to pass in review. Judgment had been passed upon my mother because of people's ignorance, especially mine. It wasn't what she did to me, but my lack of understanding as to why. I allowed myself to have those feelings and to accept the pain that had passed between us. I now saw more clearly the suffering of my own children because I, too, was dysfunctional. My mother and I had both been robbed of our childhood and youth. Now in my mid-forties, I had feelings and understanding for her! I wept for a long time, both for my mother and my children's loss too.

I don't know what I would have done without Kelly to comfort me. The first few weeks back home I spent crying for the world's indifference to suffering people.

On May 30, 1987, a black-haired, dark-eyed baby girl was laid across Carolann's tummy. Joe, the father, the new mummy and granny all hugged together and cried. Jenna the baby was Joy! Sheer joy! "God is alive and very much in control. Thank you, God! Thank you so much."

Oh God! Help me leave my wretched corpse to find the life that was born within my soul. I want to stand up and be counted as any human being does. I'm afraid, I'm so afraid to change. What if I fail?

It was my first full day at the Victoria READ Society. I had started part time in January in a one-to-one class for math while waiting for full-time classes. There were six of us. I took an instant liking to them all. Being illiterate, many of us were already broken people. Sometimes dealing with the degradation of it all seemed almost masochistic. But Melanie Austin, my first teacher, made all the difference.

Within the first six weeks of entering school, I discovered that seven million people in Canada had an education of grade eight or less. Three million couldn't read or write at all. Learning this was a devastating blow to me because I knew the pain illiteracy had caused my loved ones, and we were but one family. How could this happen in Canada? I was plagued by the question, "What can be done about it?"

The Victoria READ Society became a safe place for me because it was non-threatening. Their caring went beyond just a student's academic skills. They knew that your struggles and frame of mind had a great bearing on how well you were able to perform. They understood what it meant for us to try and access information, to walk in to a restaurant in fear of reading the menu, to read a bus schedule, to go into a bank and not feel sick to your stomach, to pretend when it comes to filling out forms that your hand was hurt or glasses broken, or guessing what the safety instructions on a medicine bottle label read.

All we learners want is what any human being wants, to have some dignity and pride, to walk down the street and feel like a whole human being, to look forward to the future and not fear it.

Education is not a privilege; it is a birthright! It is survival in a world that demands so much.

As each week passed by, and I saw more shattered lives, I gained strength to keep putting one foot in front of the other. From that energy, I also finally found the courage to confront Kelly about his drinking and ask him to move out.

After I had been at the Victoria READ School for some weeks, Linda Mitchell, the Executive Director, asked me if I would be willing to be interviewed by a reporter. I said no. The article was to promote awareness of illiteracy. Linda persisted. I relented. I'm glad I did because to my surprise, it turned out I wasn't the only one who hid my illiteracy well. Many had become experts at hiding it. In fact, the clever ways adult learners concealed their disabilities gave me an understanding that hadn't crossed my mind before: intelligence had nothing to do with learning disabilities.

Linda approached me again to be on a panel of learners, speaking to the public. Each time Linda asked me to do something like that, I'd initially say no. Then she'd say, "Yes you will, and you'll do just fine." My fear was overcome by my need to encourage other learners like myself.

By September of '88, I was attending Camosun College. What a difference from having only seven in a class; now there were over forty. Thank goodness I'd gotten my foundation of courage from the Victoria READ Society before entering a class that size. Although I was apprehensive, I was also excited. I had a volunteer tutor from Project Literacy Victoria to help me in the evenings. Having a tutor was a huge help, as I could take what I didn't understand in class and have it explained to me one-on-one, just as the Victoria READ Society had done.

The more I read, the more I learned to spell, and I began to recognize words in common places, especially in super-markets. I began to look at signs at bus stops, shop windows and any place where people wouldn't notice I was trying to read. I'd write things down and try to find them in the dictionary; that I found hard, and often got frustrated. It reminded me of when someone would say, look it up in the yellow pages. But it became a game, and the more words I recognized, the more I wanted to learn.

I studied hard, and began to ask questions with people I didn't feel threatened by, mostly my teachers. I found for me reading was an asset. I could read children's books in the privacy of my home and slowly upgrade. One evening, I read 'Red Riding Hood' and realized why that story bothered me. During the war, I wore a red suit; it was common for children to wear them at that time because, if they were lost in the bomb shelter, they would easily be recognized. Also, I was now a Grandma, and the thought of being eaten up by a wolf didn't excite me.

I also kept a journal, and all that I learned I wrote down so when I had a bad day I would read the journal to remind me how far I'd come. This helped me a lot.

That fall, I received a phone call from Anthony. He had moved to Vancouver five months previously to live with his new girl friend, Kari. They were getting married on Saturday. So Friday night we all arrived in Vancouver to stay at Anthony's house where the ceremony was to take place. The boys were downstairs, playing their music full-blast. The girls, Kim, Carolann, Kari and Heidi (my Brother Bobby's daughter), were playing cards in the kitchen while I ironed the wedding dress. We laughed all evening and it warmed my heart to see them so happy.

For a moment my memories went back to my younger years and how unhappy I'd been. It hurt, but I quickly let it go. Kari crept into my heart just as Joe had, Carolann's husband, and I was pleased Anthony had found her. The morning of the wedding started out in a rush, much like Anthony's life.

First we went to get the license. Then I went with Andy to pick up the wedding cake. It wasn't ready, and we stood there waiting for it to be iced. It was one thirty in the afternoon, and the wedding was at two o'clock. Despite the moments of panic, it came off beautifully. Kari looked stunning with her long blond hair, big, pale-blue eyes and the longest lashes I'd ever seen. I thought she was too thin, but perhaps that was the mother in me. What thrilled me most, they were planning to move to Victoria.

I was still receiving therapy, and had come to believe I was indeed a human being, worthy to be treated as such. Everything seemed so wonderful. Carolann was settled; she and the baby's father were determined to raise their own child. A new year was upon us. I wondered what it would bring, especially since I hoped to finish my grade twelve English by the end of May. I had to finish to prove to myself and my loved ones it could be done. When I thought of my granddaughter and the grandchildren to come, I was so pleased that I had gone back to school. Now, more than ever, I had to see this cruel cycle broken.

CHAPTER 16

Bring Me Flowers

M y exams were a few weeks away, and I felt very fatigued. I put it down to studying hard. At times the tiredness worried me because I felt like I was being drugged. I drank coffee and went for walks, but to no avail; my body felt drained of all energy. I kept telling myself, once the exams were over, it would pass.

As I walked home from school feeling elated, having just received a B in English, I felt sure when I phoned the doctor for my test results that they'd be the same.

As I put the phone down, I sat on the edge of my bed, stiff like a board. I could hardly breathe. All the glory of the morning had gone, crushed as though it never took place. Tomorrow I would go into the hospital and have a radical mastectomy. I thought of the five years of having been sober, my therapy with Dr. Pazder, the time I'd spent in a treatment center, the months it took for the Victoria READ Society to get me to believe in myself, how proud my children were of me. All this only to die!

I began to feel intense rage. Even if I survived, who would want to date me? But then it doesn't matter. I'll never want to date again. Now my life was over just when it was getting started.

As I arrived at the hospital with Sylvia and Kim, Linda Mitchell, Executive Director for the Victoria READ Society, was there to support me. It was then that she shared with me that she, too, was fighting cancer. She encouraged me to be strong.

When I awakened from surgery, there were flowers from everyone, my teachers from Camosun College, Victoria READ Society, Project Literacy Victoria, friends and family. Even Dr. Larry Pazder's wife and my tutor, Ruth, made a visit and dropped off flowers.

The weeks passed and I began to heal. My anger turned to strength, giving me greater hope and courage than ever before. So when I was asked to speak at a Peter Gzowski International Gold

Tournament, which raised funds for literacy, I said yes. I wasn't even tempted to say no.

On the evening of September 29, 1989, at a golf club in Victoria, I addressed an audience of over two hundred people. When I finished my speech, there was total silence. I turned to walk from the podium, and to my astonishment, people were standing, applauding me. Some surged forward to shake my hand, and I became confused. Didn't I just tell everyone how I had messed up my life and hurt others on the way? Now I was getting a standing ovation!

Peter Gzowski stood near. He was the host of the popular radio show, Morningside, and author of many books and articles for Canadian Living Magazine. He reminded me of a big, cuddly teddy bear, and I think I'll always see him that way. This wonderful man had sworn to raise one million dollars for literacy and was trekking all across the country to fulfill his promise.

When it came time to say good-bye to Peter, I was introduced to a friend of his, Robert Duncan.

He was an award-winning film and documentary producer.

As I lay awake that night still hearing the applause, I tried to understand why I felt so emotional and joyful at the same time. Then it reached me. I'd finally done something right in my life! Something, worthwhile. It was then that I knew this cancer was not going to kill me because I had too much work to do. Now I had a cause, one in which I believed. And yes! I had come to know the joys of recovery and the opportunity I'd been given. This immense gift would not be wasted and I made a promise that night to everyone who had ever suffered as I had: I would help eradicate illiteracy at every opportunity offered me.

In the months that followed, I became a board member for Project Literacy Victoria, visited the inmates at Wilkinson Road Prison and spoke on many panels with other students.

Christmas approached once again, and my children and I spent it together. Kari and Kim gave me a wonderful surprise: they were both expecting.

Early in the morning of July 8, Anthony called to say Kari was in labor and asked me to meet them at the hospital. Kari had to have an emergency caesarian. However, all went well, and Kari and Anthony had a baby girl and called her Shantelle.

On August 1, 1990, Kim gave birth to a beautiful baby boy named Jordon, and I was given prompt orders to remember his name was spelt Jordon - with no a. The first thing I did was run to the store and buy Kim a big bunch of flowers. Once again I had witnessed the miracle of life and wondered why God had changed his mind about loving me. Or had I changed my mind about Him?

The year was coming to a close, and what an extraordinary year it had been. I'd fought cancer and won. I'd had two new grandchildren. Robert had survived a car accident and was only left with scars. Sylvia had joined me in my math class. I was still seeing Dr. Pazder. I had attended Peter Gzowski's Golf Tournament for the second time and made it to my sixth A.A. birthday. I had written and read my first piece of poetry in public, learned how to type, taken a computer course, and applied for an on-the-job training program with the Victoria READ Society for the New Year. To top it off, Peter Gzowski called me to ask if he might write an article about me for the January 1991 issue of Canadian Living Magazine.

I had received more flowers this year than I ever remembered. I had chosen not to be parched and lifeless but to drink in the water that was offered: to bathe my damaged heart and give it a chance to bloom.

Little did I imagine in the year to come I would return to the desert of my childhood and stand at the gates of Warren Farm.

CHAPTER 17

Crumbling Wall

The year 1991 began with Peter Gzowski's article about me, "A Day In The Life Of A Year," published in the January issue of Canadian Living Magazine. He wrote about my illiteracy and the devastation it created in my life. It drew attention to how widespread the problem was. And due to the article, I received a phone call from Sharon McGowan, assistant to the film director Robert Duncan, wanting to interview me about the possibility of making a documentary on my life.

My first thought was much like the first interview I was asked to do with a reporter, "No", but I knew it was fear and shame that said no. I couldn't get past how I had let my children down. It was one thing to let myself down, but it was quite another when my pain hurts my innocent children. Sharon explained to me that by doing this I could help many others like me, and that was encouraging. But what would the children think?

This happened just as I started on-the-job training at the READ Society. Melanie Austin, who had been my first teacher, was now the Executive Director of the Victoria READ Society and had become a dear friend. Linda Mitchell was now Executive Director of Literacy B.C.

Sharon came to Victoria, picked me up at my home and took me out to lunch at Earl's Restaurant. She was in her thirties, had brown eyes and long, dark brown hair and a very gentle way about her. I found her very easy to talk to, and she seemed to understand my fears in making this film, yet my need to do this. I told her, if just one person found the courage to change their life from seeing my story, it would all be worthwhile. We sat in the restaurant for quite a while, and Sharon talked about my children and some of my siblings being part of the film. I was surprised at that but also pleased that my children would be given the chance to tell their own story. I discussed some of my siblings' reluctance in what I was doing and she asked,

"What do you think their fear is Ellen?"

"Although the story is about me Sharon, it is inevitable I will disclose part of their lives since we lived under the same roof as children. I understand their reluctance, although their opposition is very painful for me."

Munching on my leftover chips, I went on to say, "Although we all lived in the same house we all had our own personalities; we had our own thoughts and feelings and reacted differently to the same situation. My sister Ann was more like a mother than my mother was. She never forgot our birthdays and always made sure we had a party. And often took us to the beach or on picnics. With Billy, he was always inventing things, always trying to please my Dad and was my savior when I was in my teens. Do you know, Sharon, he once made his own steam engine? I was always fascinated at how smart he was, although he never thought so. And poor Sylvia, she was always trying to please my mum and worked so hard at it. I don't know why it never worked. So you can see why we would all react differently from one another and are at different stages in our lives. Even though I have freed myself of much denial, I still have a lot of growing to do Sharon. And I have learned that I need to accept them for who they are. It tugs at my heart just the same, but I have talked to Dr. Pazder many times about this and the answer is always the same: we all have to make our own choices, and I have made mine, Sharon."

"I hear and understand what you're saying Ellen, and I do want you to feel good about what you're doing."

"Sharon I couldn't continue life with a clear conscience if I didn't do this, knowing I have something to offer to so many hurting people? Can you imagine Sharon the damage I have done, and I am just one person? If the film touched one person's life, and gave someone the courage to turn around, how many other lives might they touch? Oh, it would all be worthwhile! But most important to me is to prove to my children how wrong I was in not having been part of their education."

Robert Duncan first filmed at my home in order to help me feel comfortable in front of the camera. Then he filmed Sylvia and me taking a walk in Beacon Hill Park. Yes! Sylvia and Billy had both agreed to be part of the documentary, and I was elated. I was also filmed at the Victoria READ Society working at my desk, with some of the students and Melanie Austin. All the children were interviewed. They filmed Billy on his boat and my friend Father William at the Franciscan Friary. We did shot in various other places in Victoria, and the rest was to be filmed in England. Filming in England would be an unforgettable experience. We were to shoot inside Warren Farm.

I arrived in England in the summer of 1991. Our first day filming, Robert, the film crew and I went down by the ocean. It was a very windy day as I stood on the beach, daring the waves to wet my shoes. As I looked up and saw the Palace Pier, the film crews' voices faded with the breaking of the waves, and I heard only the cry of the seagulls. A scene from the past flashed before me. I was a teenager standing at the end of the pier, ready to jump.

What would my death have achieved? The loss of love, which I so desperately craved, my children, my wonderful grandchildren, who all brought so much love and meaning to my life. Those comforting words that policeman spoke so long ago came back to me: "Ellen, when tomorrow comes, I promise you will feel differently."

Almost ten years had passed since I last saw my mother and, as I sat before her, I found myself struggling to find something to say. It was as though we were meeting for the first time. She had a one-room apartment, and it was very small. Her bed was off in the back of the room, and she had a big, brown chair with yellow flowers that faced the window, looking out into the street. As she sat in her chair, I noticed a small television by the window. I sat in the matching chair across from her. The room didn't have much decor to it, but Mum seemed at peace with it. Mother had finally aged. It seemed to me she was in her sixties before I ever noticed a wrinkle on her face - and then just one or two. Now she was well into her seventies and partially blind from a stroke. Her hair had turned silver, and she kept it very short. She had taken up the Catholic faith again and was going to church almost every day.

I assured Mum that if participating in the film made her feel uncomfortable, she need not take part, but Mother surprised me by saying, "I want my side of the story to be told in my own words, not someone else's."

"What is your story?" I asked her. To my dismay, she began to cry, but not like I'd ever heard her cry before. She sounded like a small child lost somewhere in the past. I felt a lump in my throat but was too uneasy to put my arms around her. Even when we had hugged each other in the past, it had been awkward and only for appearance's sake.

"Ellen; will you ever forgive me?" Mother blurted.

"For what?" I asked, knowing full well what she meant.

"I'm old now Ellen and I need to know before I die that you have forgiven me for the dreadful things I did to you."

""There's nothing to forgive, Mother," I said, lying to protect her feelings.

"Let's be honest with each other Ellen; it would help me feel better."

Realizing Mother meant what she said, I admitted to her that my childhood had been very painful, especially my teens, and I told her I had attempted suicide at fifteen. Mother showed no surprise, as though she already knew.

After talking for a while, I told Mother I truly did forgive her because I myself had experienced some of what she had suffered. I now understood her reactions to things I did or said. I also realized, through my own healing, that unlike Mother's situation, I had access to help. Those living in England in Mother's time didn't talk about emotional illness; they just passed it on to those they loved.

"It must have been hard for you during the war."

She replied that it was tough at times, but it was never as bad as when she was a child.

"Tell me about your childhood, Mother. Tell me everything you remember," I urged.

With that, we made a pot of tea that seemed to last all week.

"Some of my memories are clear, others are vague," she began. "I get confused with times and dates. However, my clearest remembrance is of feeling the shame of being poor. My father drank too much and eventually left Mother for another woman. There were seven of us children: five boys and two girls, myself and my sister Nell. We often went without a meal, and it was so cold in the winter because we couldn't afford any coal. My brothers left school as early as eleven to go to work. I left soon after. Mother didn't mind me leaving school since she agreed that education wasn't important for a woman. Furthermore, Mother thought doing housework was very good training for me for when I got married. I was a dunce in school anyway."

Mother sipped on her tea as she looked out the window, her eyes misty with tears. "Now I'm getting silly," she said and wiped her eyes with a handkerchief; I hadn't seen one of those in a while.

Mum continued, "As I became older, the shame and guilt of being poor grew. I came to believe my only hope for a better life was marriage. But who would want me? I wasn't anybody, and I had nothing. So when I met your dad, and he wanted to marry me, I said 'yes' because I was afraid I'd never be asked again."

Dear God! Hadn't I thought that way too? I'd never told anyone I felt that way, and here was mother confessing the very same. We weren't so terribly different after all. My mother's voice came back to me.

"It didn't take me long to find out your father's childhood was even worse than mine. Your dad joined the navy to escape his alcoholic stepfather. But he also admitted to me that he was afraid of what he might become if he didn't find some value to his life. He said he needed to find some dignity and reason for his being on this earth.

"Then on September 3, 1939, when your brother Billy was only three and half months old, war was officially declared. To the world's horror, World War II had begun. At first it seemed quiet, as though the war was far away. So quiet in fact, the silence was almost unbearable. Only the looks on people's faces told of war and the agony of fear for loved ones.

"When people said good-bye, some would be crying, some praying for their safe return. Sometimes I'd see service men coming home on leave, and that was wonderful. So much pain and so much love all mixed together. But when we saw the telegraph boy coming down the road on his bike, we would all hurry inside, as though it would make a difference, and he might pass by our doors if he couldn't see us. Sometimes you heard a woman scream, and even though you didn't know who it was, you would cry too for the loved one she had lost.

"It wasn't long before the war hit us all, and the sound of sirens became common. Often I'd just be going to bed, and the sirens would go off. My stomach would be tied in knots, as I'd run up the stairs calling to you children to hurry and put your coats and shoes on. Praying to God we'd make it to the shelter in time. There was the odd time I'd end up in the coal cellar instead. Your dad said it was the safest place to be if I didn't make it to the shelter on time because it was built under the stairs. That's when I could hear the bombs dropping and a thousand thoughts would pass through my mind. What if I die? Who will look after the children? If your dad were killed too, then you would be orphaned.

"Sometimes I'd catch you, Billy and Ann hiding your toys under the table because you thought it would protect them from the bombings. I couldn't even buy sweets for you children because everything was rationed. And who listened to you children cry because you were so afraid? I brought you children into this world hoping life would be kinder to you than it had been to me, and then I ended up saying 'I'm sorry' to my babies for the mess I'd brought you into."

The tears streamed down Mother's face, and every now and then she let out a big sigh. I too wanted to cry, but my tears were held back from the horrible realization of how much my mother had suffered in her life. For the first time, I was getting a clear picture of why she had reacted in so many negative ways when we children were growing up.

"Then the war was finally over! By then I had given birth to five of the seven of you. Shortly after the war, we moved to the country. Joan had been born on August 5, 1947. When we moved to Ashurst Road, I had my heart set on starting a new life. I was determined to make it work and get some sort of happiness out of all this mess. I told your father, if he really wanted to make this marriage work, he would have to leave the navy and help me bring up you children. With a new house and your dad being home, I thought it would give us a fresh start in our lives, and we'd all forget the bad times."

Forget? Isn't that why I left England? I began to swallow so hard I thought I'd choke. The tears came anyway. Here I was forty-nine years old, and I was only just beginning to truly understand what my parents had gone through. Even Dad had been born to broken dreams. I had despised my mother all these years only to discover my feelings were not much different from hers.

Mother hadn't really known what she was supposed to be in life because life had lied to her. I didn't know what I was supposed to be either. This was the first time I felt real love and compassion for my mother. Her life had been stolen from her. She never knew what being alive really meant. But saddest of all, she didn't know she had been robbed of it.

The filming of the dialogue with my mother didn't take very long, and I was very proud of her because I knew some of the questions were painful.

However, she answered them with an honesty that astonished me.

Arriving at my old school, Moulscoombe, to do some filming, I was greeted warmly by the head mistress. I felt quite emotional because as a small child I had feared this school, and now I was being treated as someone special. She had gathered all the children together in the assembly hall to sing two songs to me. It took all my will not to cry because both "Kum By Yah" and "This Is The Day The Lord Has Made" were great favorites of mine when attending school and the principal couldn't have known that. I'll never forget those little faces as they all ran up to me wanting to be hugged and kissed good-bye. After I said good-bye to the children, I sat on the wall that surrounded the playground and reflected. I noticed the bomb shelters were all sealed up. My treasure chest of memories was becoming monumental.

Arriving at Warren Farm, I was sorry Sharon had not been able to be with me while in England. I felt alone for the first time, even with the crew around. It was quiet, and I heard only the sounds of the wind. I was trying desperately to hide the abject fear I was experiencing. I felt physical pain in my stomach and realized, at the same time, I was gasping for air because I had been holding my breath. I wanted to scream out loud, "She's got to be dead by now, so why am I still afraid?"

The walls at Warren Farm were crumbling, the windows were broken and most of the white paint had peeled off the outside. Scaffolding held up some of the rotting bricks. It reminded me of some large castle I might have seen in a horror movie. But this place had been built for children. One thought was on my mind: I had to get inside to see for myself, to be very sure that these walls could no longer hurt me.

The dormitories looked smaller than I remembered them. On entering the bathroom, I was sure I could smell carbolic soap. Everything was old and broken, and the pipes were all rusted. It was so quiet. No longer could I hear the sounds that had filled this place, the children crying late at night as they lay in their beds, or in the yard outside, or the bathroom, even the dining room. This was just a dying building imprisoned in its own time, as though paying for its crimes against the innocent souls who so long ago cried out from the darkness.

Die, you bastard, die! Let this building decay, let these walls crumble and fall, never to return. Let the misery you instilled upon my siblings decompose. We have survived you, outlived your treachery and grown many seeds of love instead.

As these thoughts ran through my head, I knew in my heart it was Miss Salad that I so badly wanted to say this to. Yes, time had passed, but not all wounds healed because the memories refuse to leave until my demise.

Having finished the filming, I went back to the dormitory on my own, to take a last look at where my bed had once been. A black crucifix still hung upon the wall. The recollections of that time long past would never be forgotten, but at last, at long last, I was able to lay them to rest in the happiness of my new life. People say, tomorrow never comes, but tomorrow has arrived. It is here now! It is in all of my children and grandchildren, all of my teachers, tutors, those wonderful students whose classes I shared, Peter Gzowski, Robert Duncan, and so many wonderful friends, even my doctors, Judy Fries and Lawrence Pazder, none of whom I knew on that lonely summer night. They were all strangers then; yet in time, they helped remove the shackles of my life and set me free, bringing even greater promises of tomorrow.

CHAPTER 18

The Power of Love

The two weeks in England went by so quickly, and all too soon I was on a plane heading back home. It had been quite an experience but a good one. I was able to put closure on a sad time so long ago. And best of all, I had discovered my mother.

Back at the READ Society in Victoria, I continued with my on-the-job training program. We were to receive a pay cheque every two weeks, which meant I was no longer on welfare. That was a marvelous feeling. At long last I was independent and a taxpayer contributing to my country Canada. I felt so proud.

During the months of life skills training, I did a lot of public speaking. I spoke to social workers, educators, government officials, adult learners in class, and the public in general; I spoke at Wilkinson Road Prison, colleges and various organizations – anywhere we might find people willing to listen. I wrote poetry and read it at various functions. One piece, 'The Wind Cannot Read,' was published in a book of students' writings. The book was named after my poem. I also wrote a short story called "How Do We See Street People?" It was published in another book of student writings.

With all that was going on in my life, it never occurred to me just how much I had grown. Only a few years before, I had been on welfare with a serious drinking problem, going nowhere fast. Now I was going somewhere so quickly I hadn't slowed down to find out where. Perhaps I was afraid to stop and think about what I had accomplished in such a short period of time. I might get frightened and run back into the shell it took me so many years to escape from.

What I had learned from it all was that there are many adult learners with incredible talents who have much to offer the world but are afraid to show it. People like this give me the courage to continue trying to help others come out of the grayness of their lives. Bloody hell, life is too damn short not to let the world know you're here.

On New Year's Eve 1990, I received a phone call asking me to start work as a receptionist at the Royal Bank. Imagine me! Working at a bank!

Fireworks exploded into radiant colors above Victoria's inner harbor. The historic Empress Hotel, the parliament building and all the boats were lit up as the music of Auld Lang Syne filled the air. I stood alone on the bow of my brother Billy's boat and gave a silent prayer of thanks. Oh, how I had changed. This great country of mine, Canada, had given me a new life, a reason for being, my independence and so many friends. And best of all, I have four Canadian children and five Canadian grandchildren whom I love so very much. Thank you, Canada.

Early in spring of 1991 'Ellen's Story' aired throughout North America and in many parts of the world.   When I first watched it on television, Pink Floyd's song "The Wall" haunted me.   It was as though I was trying to reassure myself that it was truly over, that my walls had crumbled. With the fallen bricks, I could build a new foundation for my life and family. I received some wonderful mail and phone calls from teachers throughout B.C, friends from Vancouver, Victoria and even Montreal. I even had people stop me in the street, and it warmed my heart as many were adult learners. Most important of all, my children were proud of me. However, I knew I had only grazed the surface and that there was still much work to be done.

Opportunities to speak grew over the course of the year. Then Linda Mitchell called me from Vancouver. The B.C. Broadcaster's Association was giving a Humanitarian Award of one million dollars of free advertising for an organization they felt was needy. Would I represent learners and Literacy BC by giving a speech to their panel in the New Year? Nine different organizations would apply by giving a presentation. The moment I put the phone down that sick feeling hit me. "You'll screw it up and let all those learners down." This was one time I had to let go and let God take care of it and just give it all I had.

On January 14, 1992, I represented literacy learners throughout British Columbia before a panel of broadcasters. Everyone there seemed so official in his or her suits; however, Linda was there to support me. As I told my story, the tears began to flow because I was experiencing not only my own pain but also that of so many others like me, and I was so fearful of failing these people.

I heard myself saying to the audience: "The demand for higher literacy skills is growing as never before due to our changing world of technology and the need to compete on a global level. This helped me realize there was a greater need for public awareness than ever before. If people did not come together to tear down the walls of illiteracy, this country would have more people living with rage than calm, more bitterness than we can console, despair instead of hope, lack of self-confidence leading to distrust, and mass confusion leaving little or no respect for order, leading even to emotional disorder, chemical abuse and violence." I then went on to tell them a true story about a single mother of four, and only at the end did I tell them that mother was me!

On the following Monday, Linda phoned. Literacy BC had won the Humanitarian Award. I leaned up against the wall, staring at a photograph of my grandchildren, allowing the tears to roll down my face. The more students I listened to, the more I recognized the tragedy of illiteracy.

In 1993, Robert Duncan received the Golden Sheaf Award at the Chicago Film Festival and the Silver Award in Houston, Texas for "Ellen's Story."

After the release of the film I spoke to many groups; high schools, adult learners, universities, social clubs, colleges, women's groups, and conferences on learning difficulties. I wrote articles for newspapers and had my poetry published. I received an award from the English Speaking Union for my work in literacy. And in 1994, I received the Flight For Freedom Award from the Governor

General of Canada, Ramon John Hnatyshyn. On hearing about the award, tears of elation streamed down my face. I knew the truth. My Flight For Freedom Award belonged to a world of people who had taken the courage to carve their lives to a new design and to find the dignity and pride which rightfully belongs to all.

Many friends and teachers encouraged me to fill in the missing pieces from the documentary and write a book. I had long ago dreamed of writing but was robbed of the ambition because I believed what others told me: I was dumb and would never amount to anything. However, as I began to write my book, it seemed all was well, and I had found a purpose to life and was feeling very much alive. For a while the world seemed to be a far better place, and the pain arose only once in a while. I never expected it to go away completely, but I thought I'd had my share and now there would be some peace in my life.

In 1994, I received a phone call to say Kelly was dead; the light in my heart went out for a long time. Eighteen months later my mother died and my brother Billy followed her two weeks later, dying of cancer. Sixteen months later my Brother Bobby's only daughter Heidi and all four of her children were murdered. The writing of my book was left to collect dust. I remembered a song from my childhood days, "Run, rabbit, run rabbit, run, run, run, here comes the farmer with his gun, gun, gun." I was very frightened, and it seemed as though there was no place to hide. The pain my family shared in those first few months following the death of Heidi and her children no one could understand.

When the year 2001 began, I picked up my book and started again. Why? I knew more than ever before, that life is a love affair with humankind, and every moment is a gift. Sometimes anxiety rears its head, but I look forward to tomorrow and know that whatever it brings, it can't bring back the sorrows of yesterday. My grandmothers suffered so much, yet they carried on sacrificing for the love of their children. My parents never knew what it was to own their own home, a car, telephone, fridge, stove, washer, dryer or even to take a vacation. All my parents ever knew was to work until they dropped so they might feed and clothe their children. Both my mother and father, as children, knew what it was to go hungry, and they swore this would not happen to their own. It did not. They survived a war as my grandmothers did before them, and were expected to carry on as though all was the same as before. To say they came out un-changed, would be a lie. Wars changes lives forever and no one wins.

It is the power of love that allows one to pick up the pieces and continue. I stayed in denial for far too long and almost went to my death on a lie. I can't turn the clock back, but I can move forward in the grace and beauty I know my life was meant to be. There may be more pain to come in my life, but there will also be the joy of having learned about the power of love. It has carried me through many, heartaches and taken me to the heavens, giving me joys I did not know possible. However, it's much more than just the honor and privilege of being a parent and grandparent, it's about someone loving you for who you are, expecting nothing in return.

That's the real power! What joy there is in the hearts of those who sacrifice to find love within the lifetime they have? There are so many people helping others whose names will never be heard or found in a history book. Often, when awakening to the breaking of the dawn, I lie in bed and wonder how many will awaken to darkness. If only I could reach out and touch them all, they would learn that the darkness that was once in my life became the illumination of my new found being because somebody cared.

It is because someone cared that I have been sober for twenty-five years, healed many wounds, fought cancer and have my grade twelve. I am now a qualified counselor for grief and loss. I have volunteered for twenty years in the field of literacy with adult learners, helped raise funds for children with learning difficulties, sat on eight boards for literacy organization, wrote to students who needed help or just provided a listening ear. But most important of all, I am a proud mother of four children and a very proud grandmother of five.

Through the blackness of my life to the light of new growth, I realize love comes with a great deal of courage. To those who have suffered I say this, love can be found among the ruins as I myself found it. I have seen its brilliance in the many rooms of Alcoholics Anonymous, among the adult learners, in class and in teachers who never give up hope on students. There are those who welcome volunteer tutoring, with their endless patience and energy. Finally, I have seen it in my family, whose love was so abundant. They made me what I am today, they held me up to be counted and they waited believing in me until the time came when I could tilt my own face toward the sky and breathe my own sigh.

The Wind Cannot Read

I want to be like the wind. It cannot read.

The wind will sail a ship to shore bringing Food, to feed the poor, bringing smiles to a child's face as he blows their kites into Place no matter what color, creed or race. Yet the wind cannot read.

The wind can fly as high as a mountain while I dream to read as I sit by the fountain. My heart is of great sorrow and I already dread, the coming, of tomorrow. I am imprisoned, yet the wind, cannot read.

The wind will fly, a bird through the sky, blow great colors, of the changing seasons, while I still agonize to reason. Where is my freedom? While the wind flies books of joy to many places, for me, they bring great fear and disgraces. Yet the wind cannot read.

The wind is loved and respected by many, seen by None, felt by all, seems so strong and seems so tall. Me, I just feel very small.

"Ho" God could you teach me to read? Then I could be free. Take away my sorrow and, let me see. "Come child, come ride with me. I will teach you to read, and set you free, for I am the wind."

The Beginning

ISBN 1425121297-2